Consider
the Birds

Books by Callie Smith Grant

The Cat on My Lap
The Dog at My Feet
The Cat in the Window
The Dog Next Door
The Horse of My Heart
Second-Chance Dogs
The Horse of My Dreams
Second-Chance Cats
The Dog Who Came to Christmas
The Cat in the Christmas Tree
Second-Chance Horses

Consider the Birds

Heartwarming True Stories
of Our feathered friends

Edited by
Callie Smith Grant

Revell

a division of Baker Publishing Group
Grand Rapids, Michigan

Published by Revell
a division of Baker Publishing Group
Grand Rapids, Michigan
RevellBooks.com

Printed in the United States of America

Library of Congress Cataloging-in-Publication Data
Names: Grant, Callie Smith editor
Title: Consider the Birds : Heartwarming True Stories of Our Feathered Friends / [edited by] Callie Smith Grant.
Description: Grand Rapids, Michigan : Revell, a division of Baker Publishing Group, [2025]
Identifiers: LCCN 2025001158 | ISBN 9780800740955 paperback | ISBN 9780800747459 | ISBN 9781493451449 ebook
Subjects: LCSH: Birds—Religious aspects—Christianity | Birds—Social aspects | Human-animal relationships
Classification: LCC BR115.B55 B57 2025 | DDC 636.6—dc23/eng/20250709
LC record available at https://lccn.loc.gov/2025001158

Baker Publishing Group publications use paper produced from sustainable forestry practices and postconsumer waste whenever possible.

"Lindy Says Hello" was previously published in Kings River Life.

25 26 27 28 29 30 31   7 6 5 4 3 2 1

In loving memory of Lonnie Hull DuPont—
Poet, Author, Editor, Musician,
Teacher, Mentor, Friend, Animal Lover.
Always in our thoughts, her eternal love is a blessing to us all.

Contents

Contents

Contents

A Note from the Editor

Callie Smith Grant loved telling stories. I knew Callie first by her real name, Lonnie Hull DuPont, a veteran of the publishing industry when I entered the field over thirty years ago. For more than twenty years, we worked together (separately, because we both telecommuted) at Baker Publishing Group. Seven times a year, we all gathered in Grand Rapids for various meetings. And there were many conventions and conferences too. Lonnie could hold dinner tables spellbound and keep us rolling with laughter as she'd regale us with story after story. I miss her laugh and I miss those stories.

Lonnie loved stories. Many years ago, she asked me about gathering a collection of dog—and maybe cats, please?—stories. Cats because, you know, there are more cats with humans as staff than there are dog owners. Publishers have certain rules, and one of ours at the time was "We don't do well with story collections." We're all glad we put that rule aside, with now a dozen books and hundreds of thousands of copies sold. Lonnie, writing under the pen name of Callie, loved to point out that the cat books often sold more than the dog books.

Lonnie also loved collecting stories. Every few years, she'd call or email and say, "Is it time for another couple of books? Maybe horses this time?" Or, "How about rescued animals? Those would be great stories." And, like Topsy, the story collections grew. Lonnie would enlist another merry band of storytellers who delivered more heartwarming stories readers enjoyed. And I, or Madame Editor as "Callie" addressed me in emails, have been privileged to be on the team for all of them.

Lonnie loved her authors. Both those who wrote stories for her animal books under Callie's name and those who knew her as Lonnie. She guided each of them with wisdom honed from years in the publishing biz and loved them and their projects passionately.

And Lonnie loved you, readers. You were always front of mind as she gathered and often penned stories for her animal-themed collections. She knew your passion for animals, both in general and specifically for dogs, cats, horses, and now . . . birds.

I'm writing this editor's note one year from the day that Lonnie left us. This collection of stories about birds was a passion project for her. As her publisher, we were slow to come on board, and now, though she chose all the final stories before we lost her, we're bringing this book to completion without her gentle, deft hand at the wheel. Callie had one hard and fast rule for all of her animal books. The stories could never be about the death of an animal. But for this one, Lonnie chose to include some. I still feel a bit awkward breaking that rule here as now we soldier on without her. Thank you, readers, for being loyal fans of these story collections. And Callie, uh, Lonnie . . . thanks for crafting these story collections that have meant so much to so many readers.

Lonnie, you were right all along . . . people love stories.

Vicki Crumpton
August 1, 2024

one

Alberta

LONNIE HULL DuPONT

It was on the first of May that my husband Joe and I heard strange noises from under the yew bushes next to our patio. It was a lovely spring day, the day before the birthday of my stepfather—the man who raised me and who had died only three months before.

This was a noise we didn't recognize. Joe peered through the bushes. "It's a chicken," he announced.

"A chicken?" I found this hard to believe. Yes, we lived in the country, but there were no chickens in the immediate vicinity.

"It's a chicken, all right. It's little and black." Joe paused. "Should we feed it?"

"I guess so, but I'm not sure what chickens eat," I said. I knew they liked to pick things off the ground, but that was about it. I went indoors and rustled up some unsalted peanuts and unpopped popcorn, and the hen did indeed come forth and eat.

We sat and watched her. She was tiny, raven black, with a deep red comb that extended in red leathery seams into her face. I've never been one to notice chickens particularly, but we both agreed she was very pretty.

And hungry. And noisy. She clucked away and looked at us and waddled around us as we sat on the patio. We decided to call her Alberta after my stepdad Al, not only because his birthday was the following day but also because he had bought his first Model T with a box of banty hens. And because he would not eat poultry.

I figured that somehow Alberta had wandered off her farm, wherever it may be, and that she would return to it. I didn't expect her to be with us the next day. But there she was, sitting quietly on the patio, waiting to be fed. I called my sister and brother-in-law to ask about proper food, and they supplied us with a big bag of chicken feed.

In the meantime, I was immersed in a fairly hard depression. Many months later I would learn it was from a physical ailment, and I found successful treatment for that ailment. But at the time, I decided that I would try gardening to help my state of mind. I kept it simple, buying only a few things at the nursery. But the initial planting seemed overwhelming. A few days after Alberta arrived, I sat down on the patio steps and began to cry.

I sensed a little presence at my feet. I opened my eyes, and there stood Alberta, cocking her head at me. She had food, so apparently she was standing near me because she simply wanted to. I started talking to her while she cocked her head back and forth. I began that day a tradition of talking to her as if she could understand me. She was wonderful company—a bright spot in a difficult time.

After it was clear that the initial work of putting in the garden was too much for me, I hired a couple college guys to help. Alberta joined us in our work. Every time the guys dug up a worm, they'd toss it to her, and she'd catch it midair. She ate well that day. And now I had a garden where Alberta and I could putter. I don't know a lot about chickens. Maybe they're all this sociable. But Alberta loved to hang around people. We had my mother's eightieth birthday party on the patio a week after Alberta's arrival, and that morning in preparation for the party, Joe raked up winter's leftovers for three hours. Alberta followed him around the yard, sometimes perching on the yew bushes, sometimes bobbing contentedly nearby in the grass. When the guests arrived, she mingled with them, a complete hit. Everyone fell in love with her.

All summer Alberta stayed. We fed and watered her and found her eggs here and there. Although the side patio and its yew bushes were her home, if we missed a feeding or were too late, she would walk around the house, up the front steps, and cluck up such a racket at the front door that our house cat was simply beside herself. And Alberta would get her breakfast, pronto.

Eventually both Joe and I found ourselves talking to her. She was almost eating out of Joe's hand. I would often sit on the patio steps and watch her edge closer to me yet keep a little distance. I cooed over her, told her my problems. I prayed while sitting out there, so grateful was I that this little bird came along to distract me from my darkness.

The part of Michigan where we lived has coyotes and any number of other wild things that could hurt Alberta. But she stayed safe. Nevertheless, we knew that when cold weather hit, she could not survive without shelter. So we put the word out: Would someone like a pet hen and not eat her?

Someone would. My niece and her family lived about ten miles away and were willing to take Alberta to add to their growing menagerie. We really didn't want to give her up, but we knew it was necessary. It was now the end of summer, and I was on the mend. Still, I hated to let my little chicken go.

On Alberta's last day with us, we sat outside and told her where she was going and why. We put some feed in the bottom of a laundry basket on its side. She waddled around it, then walked in and began to eat. We slowly righted the basket and put a lid on it, then drove to my niece's. Sure enough, there were pets galore there—in particular, one fat, friendly hen named Goldilocks who would become Alberta's best friend.

Today Alberta runs around a big backyard with Goldilocks. Their wings are unclipped so they can fly from danger, and they lay eggs wherever they wish. At night the two of them roost in a shed protected by a noisy billy goat who really likes them. I expect Alberta to live a good life.

As for me, I'm back to myself. The world is a wonderful place again for me. I continue in the knowledge that God made the creatures of the earth for good reasons. And I believe in particular that he created a lovely black banty hen and delivered her to me to get me through that hard summer. I am forever grateful.

two

That Day My Husband Cut Down a Tree

SUSY FLORY

One of the best and most surprising moments of my life involved the sudden materialization of a flock of birds. It was a beautiful summer day at our northern California house on the western slope of the Sierra Nevada mountains. We live on the top of a ridge surrounded by a healthy forest full of trees such as ponderosa pines, incense cedars, Douglas firs, and black oaks, some of them so big it can take three people linking hands to get their arms around the trunk. The trees make a person feel small and humble.

Then there are the smaller trees—mountain dogwood, hazelnut, buckeye, laurel, big leaf maple (so gorgeous in the fall, with a single leaf big enough to cover your face and then some), and madrone. All of the trees in our part of the forest intermingle, and sometimes they even grow together at the root or trunk level, like conjoined twins.

The day the flock pulled off the magic trick, I was sitting in the front garden, about a quarter acre enclosed by a wire fence to keep out the deer (but not the squirrels, who regularly raid the poor vegetable plants we try to grow). I soaked in the sunshine and smiled at the butterflies as I looked around the garden, the lavender buzzing with bees and little white berries on the snowberry plant gleaming in the sun.

Gradually my eyes rose up to the Douglas fir tree next to the garden shed. It's a younger fir but still twenty-five or thirty feet high, and I saw some movement deep inside the branches. I looked closer, trying to focus, and all at once the tree burst to life like a 3D movie, branches and needles quivering. Out of the tree from every possible angle burst a flock of small birds, like popcorn popping out of a pan. The birds leapt up into the air in a loosely organized group, spreading out as they took wing and then circled above me. After a lap or two, they slowed and came gliding down into the garden. I was stunned by the surprise, by the sight and the feel of it, the warm summer air left vibrating from the wingbeats and the air they'd displaced all around me.

I sat still as could be, trying not to move or even breathe as the birds settled into and across the garden, hopping about and pecking at tiny things on the ground. The mixed flock of juncos, white-crowned sparrows, red-breasted nuthatches, mountain chickadees, and spotted towhees took turns visiting the feeder over by the wild plum tree or sitting on the edge of the birdbath, waiting their turn for a dunk and splash. The birds were going about their business, not noticing me or maybe even just ignoring me.

Although I've seen mixed flocks many times since then, this was my very first experience, and in my mind's eye I replayed the moment: One second there had been no birds, and the next the tree had spit dozens of them out into the air. Where had they come from? Had the birds snuck into the fir when I wasn't looking? Or had they been hiding or sleeping inside and waiting for just the right time to emerge? I thought about how important the trees are to the birds here; not only do they provide food, nesting spots, and shade, but they are also stops on the avian highway, a safe place to rest and to hide. I've always loved our trees and had been known to hug one here or there, but this peek into the relationship between a tree and these birds made me love trees even more.

This might explain why, when my husband walked into the house one Saturday red-faced and sweating and announced, "I just cut down the tree by the well pump," I instantly felt a pang.

"What tree?!"

We have no shortage of trees, but they feel almost like children to me. Even if it was a problem tree and needed to be removed for some reason, I was already feeling sad about it. I needed to know what tree he had cut down.

"The scrubby one with the red peeling bark," he said. "It was too close to the pump." He smiled; he was keeping our water source safe.

I started chewing a fingernail, my mind racing. When it came to cutting up dead trees for firewood, I was all for it. But living trees? Not so much. I also knew my husband didn't like manzanitas or deer brush, which, even though they are native plants, are considered weeds by those who view them as a fire hazard. But I didn't think we had any on the property. I decided to take a walk down to the well pump and see for myself. My daughter, a zoology major and ecologist who works in wildlife rescue, went with me. She loves trees even more than I do.

Down at the pump, we bent down and examined the remains of the tree. It turned out not to be a manzanita after all but a six- to seven-foot-tall madrone tree.

Ouch! I thought, my heart hurting more than a little.

Madrones are beautiful, multi-trunked trees with smooth greenish trunks that seem to glow from within. When you touch them, they feel cold even on a hot day, like a cold bottle of soda from the refrigerator. Overlaying the trunk is a reddish, rough skin that peels up in curls, inviting you to pull off a small, loose piece. The canopy is composed of gracefully fluttering green leaves that turn flame-red in the fall, making the madrone a gracious and beautiful tree that stands out like a gem among the evergreens.

Madrones grow in a narrow elevation band across the Sierras and are almost impossible to cultivate, so you mostly only see them in the wild. They grow slowly, and so each individual madrone, including this one, feels precious. When you cut a madrone down, you are cutting down and destroying a living organism that is an important part of the environment, a link in a beautiful and important chain. So, of course we gave my husband a hard time.

"Promise me you'll tell us next time you want to cut down a tree," I said as our daughter Teddy explained, in detail, the difference between a manzanita and a madrone. "Robert, I really love madrones. Have you ever felt their trunks?"

He knows us. He understood. Properly contrite, he agreed to talk over future tree removal strategies, then ate his lunch and went back down to take away the poor madrone's branches.

Later I looked at the carnage, and all that was left was a three-lobed stump. I was very sad for a few days, but of course my husband hadn't done it on purpose, and we had lots of other trees to think about and enjoy, including a few small madrones along the front. Eventually I forgot about it.

A year later, Teddy brought home a bird. Her job involved taking care of injured and orphaned birds at the wildlife center bird nursery, but from time to time she brought a bird home to go into an outdoor flight cage to strengthen its wings in preparation for eventual release into the forest.

This particular bird was a spotted towhee, about the size of a robin, like some of those I'd seen in the garden. The males are black on top with bright white wing spots, reddish sides, and a white belly. This bird was a female, much lighter in color and with more blended markings, making her harder to spot as she hopped around the bottom of her carrier. I noticed how one of her wings hung down a bit; Teddy said she'd been retrieved from the mouth of a cat and had come into the center with a broken wing. She was doing much better, although the wing was still a little weak.

Wildlife rescue is still in its infancy with many kinds of animals, as most attention has gone toward wolves, bears, bison, eagles, and other high-profile wildlife dearly loved by the public. But the average bird or squirrel has not gotten the same attention, care, and research as these celebrity species. To remedy this problem, a vast army of wildlife rescuers and their organizations have spontaneously formed across the globe over the last decade or two and are pioneering all sorts of treatments for all sorts of creatures, including those like this little unassuming towhee. In the past, a broken wing would have been an automatic death sentence, but not anymore. Wildlife folks have figured out how to mend many seemingly unmendable things, and so this girl's wing had been set and was healing. There was every reason to believe the towhee would be fine and head back to the forest within a few months, as she was already flying at about three-quarters normal capacity. Her future was bright.

The afternoon Teddy brought the towhee home, I went out with her to help with the transfer into the aviary, and I admired the little brown bird who had survived the cat, a fearsome predator to wild birds. My job was to open and shut the door of the aviary while Teddy handled the bird and got her inside.

21

As usual we coordinated our efforts, but this time, something went wrong. The quiet little towhee exploded into the air just as Teddy was carefully lowering her down through the door, and she burst up and through the crack and took flight, flapping fiercely as she banked and headed down toward the back woods. She was flying about two feet above the ground, a bird on a mission.

"Mom!" Teddy yelled. "We have to get her. She's not ready yet."

In that same moment, out of the corner of my eye, I saw a bright orange and white streak of something flash by, heading in the same direction.

"Mom!" Teddy screamed. "It's Baby Girl!"

My heart dropped. Baby Girl was our barn cat, a beautiful feral calico cat that had been unadoptable at the local humane society due to a bad attitude. She had been adopted three times, and each time she had been returned. She had once bitten the director on the hand. So Baby Girl ended up in the barn cat program, where cats who disliked humans could find a comfortable home and return the favor to the human who hosted them by keeping the mouse population in check. We'd been having a mouse problem in our large, sunny garage, and so we'd taken Baby Girl in. We left her alone for the first year or so, and she hid out for a while, but lately she had emerged for the occasional pet or treat. Even so, the fluffy calico still had a wild streak and probably always would.

On this day, Baby Girl apparently escaped from an open door on the side of the garage, and unbeknownst to us had been sunning herself on the deck. She'd probably watched with interest as Teddy carried the carrier into the backyard, and she must have tiptoed down the deck stairs to watch. When the bird unexpectedly escaped, Baby Girl had taken off like a rocket, and now the little bird was in grave danger.

We both screamed as we ran after the cat and the bird, which was still flying low and awkwardly along the ground. "Baby Girl! Baby Girl! Stop . . . stop!" To her credit, she seemed to listen and shifted into a lower gear, trotting along, seemingly enjoying the pursuit. Panting, we caught up to her, but by now there was no bird in sight.

Baby Girl stopped and then sauntered over to the well pump, where she walked up to a small bush and peered into it. We shooed her away and she walked a few steps and sat down to watch.

Where was the bird? Baby Girl didn't have her. Where was she?

Then Teddy spotted her, deep inside the green leafy bush. The frightened towhee was in the back, moving around a bit from branch to branch but well hidden. We considered what to do. We had a loose bird and a feral cat to deal with.

"Go get a towel, Mom. We have to get Baby Girl back inside."

I quickly ran and grabbed a towel from the house, handing it to Teddy. Even though Baby Girl had gotten friendlier, I was still afraid of tooth and claw, but Teddy had a way. She gathered her up and carried the excited cat back up to the garage while I stayed and watched the little bird tucked safe inside the bush.

While I was staring into the shadows and trying to keep an eye on her, I looked at the little branches and leaves that grew out of a three-lobed green stump that seemed to glow from within and felt a shock.

It was the madrone tree!

In the year since my husband had cut down the tree, the stubborn and very-much-alive madrone had apparently been busy sprouting back up again. Instead of the original three trunks, it was now something like ten or fifteen shoots growing up from the stump, each bearing dozens of beautiful green leaves that quivered a little whenever the bird moved around inside. What

I thought was dead was very much alive, the old roots nurturing new growth. The recovering tree was easily two or three times the volume it had been before, although it was still only a few feet high. I could not believe it.

Then Teddy was back, and although she tried her best to capture the bird, the little towhee was too deep inside and apparently determined to be free. After a few tense minutes, the bird lifted up and out of the madrone and flew off into the deep forest behind our house. She flew slowly and seemed a little unsteady, but she could definitely fly.

There was no way Teddy could catch her, so together we stood in the waning light of the day and watched her fly away until we couldn't see her anymore, hoping and praying she would find a safe place to roost and continue to heal. We gave her back to the forest as one must do in this kind of work. It was where she belonged and where she would be most happy. The forest was calling her, and she had listened.

We walked back toward the house, stopping again at the madrone. I thought about Robert that day the year before, and how upset I'd been that he had cut down the tree. But if he hadn't previously cut it down, the bird wouldn't have had a safe place to land. She might have fallen into the clutches of Baby Girl in a second cat attack, likely a fatal encounter this time.

Cutting the tree had removed the main trunk, but it had also stimulated the old roots into fresh and rapid growth, making it a perfect place—like a small bushy shrub—for the towhee to hide away and be safe. The old mature trunk could not have sheltered the bird. So one life had been traded for another, and what seemed like death had instead become a resurrection and rebirth.

I hope the towhee found the mixed flock and joined it and maybe even now she's out there flitting among the trees, bursting forth with the flock from the darkness into the light, and using that healed-up wing to rise up on the warm air. Maybe she occasionally stops by the madrone, still flourishing in this second stage of its own wild life, or maybe she just bypasses it altogether for bigger, taller, safer trees. She belongs to the forest again, her true home, and Teddy continues the work. Each life precious, each recovery a miracle.

three

How Matty Became Brave

ALLISON LYNN FLEMMING

Matty and Charlie were quite the duo—two happy budgies sharing a branch in a little white cage, brought together by design.

You see, my first budgie, Prince, had only lived two years. My parents decided that, despite all my love, he must have been lonely. So this time around, we were getting a pair. We spent an hour at the pet store, marveling at the brightly colored birds. Their musical chirps filled the store with boisterous joy. They flitted about the large cage, vying playfully for our attention. Any of them would have been wonderful pets, but we were looking for something special. We wanted to find two happy little guys who could become friends, maybe even brothers.

Charlie's bright turquoise chest and happy song caught my attention. He was animated and friendly. Matty's plumage was a warm violet, with a spot of orange above his beak. He was gentle, shy even, but curious. Both birds had fully striped heads, showing their youth. If we got them now, they could grow up together, making each other happy for years to come.

We excitedly brought them home and got them settled. After just a few days, Charlie's and Matty's personalities really began to show. Charlie was spirited and outgoing—the extrovert of the pair! He chirped and came to the front of the cage whenever anyone entered the room. He made sure he was first in line when treats were around and let us know if he wanted for anything. There was no doubt about it—Charlie was in charge!

Matty was larger than Charlie, with a serene presence. Despite his dominant size, Matty was quite comfortable letting Charlie take the reins. When we opened the cage to let them fly around the kitchen, Charlie bravely flew out while Matty cautiously stepped just outside the bars. When we started to teach them tricks, Charlie took the lead, allowing Matty to learn from him. Charlie acted like the protective big brother, taking all the scary first steps. All Matty had to do was follow. They were a perfect little pair.

For years, they lived together in fraternal harmony. But one morning, we came downstairs to a heartbreaking sight. Charlie was lying still in the bottom of the cage. Matty was sitting far in the back, curled up against the side of the bars. We saw our own grief reflected in Matty's stiff and sad posture. We wondered how he would survive without his fearless best friend.

As the weeks unfolded, we paid special attention to Matty. We held him on our finger as often as possible and encouraged him to take treats from our hands.

But soon, our family faced another transition—we were moving. My dad had been offered a job in another province. The cross-country travel would be too much for our little Matty. He'd already been through so much change!

Mom started making calls and quickly found him a new home with a loving family. We gave them a gentle warning, "He's already several years old, and he just lost his best friend. We don't know how much strength he has left in him."

The family understood and promised to care for him with gentleness and peace.

Well, none of us were prepared for what was going to happen next.

Matty didn't just survive—he started to thrive!

It was like he'd received a fresh start. His new environment didn't have the memories of Charlie and their time together. Instead, this was his home, his place to shine. Bit by bit, he started to explore and enjoy his new world.

He started coming to the side of the cage for treats and eagerly jumped on anyone's finger. He loved sitting at the side of his cage to have a little "visit" with human guests. And his voice! All of a sudden, Matty was chirping and singing up a storm!

We all knew Matty had loved Charlie, but Charlie was a huge personality. With him gone, it was like Matty had found a courage all his own. In learning to live by himself, he had discovered the joy of trying new things and connecting with the world on his own terms.

Our once fearful Matty had learned to be brave.

Matty's new family sent regular messages about his steady progress and his growing sense of adventure. Across the country, I became Matty's cheerleader! As a shy teenager, I found that his newfound courage resonated deeply with me. As I started to explore our new city, with all its dreams and challenges, I, too, was learning to be brave. Who knew a feathery little creature could provide so much inspiration?

Over the years, our updates on Matty became fewer and far between. Our sweet, timid budgie had found a happy life. Each Christmas, his new family included a little update about Matty in their family newsletter. We were thrilled to know he was doing so well.

One day, we received a phone call—Matty had peacefully passed away in his sleep. It was the end of an era. Even though we hadn't seen him in many years, we still shed a few tears and lifted a prayer of gratitude.

Our shy little Matty—the one we thought wouldn't last a day without Charlie—lived for a whopping ten years.

But it wasn't just about the number of years—it was about what he did with that time. Matty learned to step outside his comfort zone and accept the love and guidance of a new family. He found the courage to try new things and a fuller life than any of us had imagined for him.

For years, as I struggled under my own shyness, I thought, *I'm Matty, but I wish I was like Charlie.* But then I realized that being Matty was pretty awesome too. Charlie was who he was—exciting, fun, and naturally filled with joy. But Matty was strong. He pushed through and conquered his fears, without ever losing his sweet, gentle spirit.

And along the way, he taught us all a beautiful lesson: Be brave.

God created all of us—even the smallest little pieces of creation—to live with confidence and joy. It's okay to follow others, but never let fear hold you back from discovering and enjoying the full life God has planned for you.

For such a tiny little creature, Matty left a large legacy of courage and love.

four

The Robin's Nest

KATELYN VAN KOOTEN

Four blue eggs, as beautiful as polished turquoise, lay cradled in the basket-like nest in the crook of the crabapple tree. I balanced on a large landscaping rock, craning my neck to admire them.

I might not have found the nest if I hadn't spent so much time walking that spring. It was April of 2020, and the rhythms of my life had been jarred into something unfamiliar. My Twitter feed was full of reports of the Covid-19 virus spreading daily, with cases being reported closer and closer to my home in Michigan. I was unemployed, church had become a weekly video on my laptop screen, and it wasn't safe to see my friends. I felt like I had nothing to do but sit at home and fret about the state of the world, bogged down in my loneliness and fear of an uncertain future.

One of the ways I coped was going for walks as often as the weather allowed, letting the daylight and blooming flowers clear my head, looking at the sidewalk chalk rainbows left by the neighbors' kids, listening to the birds sing, connecting with the world beyond my house.

The crabapple tree shaded a flower bed at the intersection of our driveway and the sidewalk, so I passed it every time I left to loop around the neighborhood or walk to the park. Often, there was an American robin in the tree when I passed. She'd chirp an alarm at my approach, but she wouldn't fly away when I rounded the low-hanging branches, or when I spent an afternoon weeding around the impatiens under her perch.

One of those days, I spotted the nest, half-hidden where the trunk began to split into branches, creating a haven just the right size for a bird's nest. I needed just a little more height to see inside, and the big, decorative rocks along the back of the flower bed were the perfect step stool.

And there they were, those four blue eggs, like drops of sky collected in a space about the size of my cupped hands.

Their mother fussed at me from a budding branch above them.

"Sorry to bother you," I whispered back. "I don't mean any harm, I promise."

But I bothered her over and over during the following weeks; I couldn't help myself. Those days were heavy with constant news of economic disaster, overwhelmed hospitals, and an ever-rising death toll—but checking on the robin eggs never failed to give me a little flutter of joy.

Near the end of April, I sneaked onto the big, flat viewing rock to see that the gemlike eggs were gone. In their place was a huddle of chicks, fuzzy and fragile. They weren't exactly cute yet, with their ungainly proportions and patchy down, but they were beautiful. I held my breath as they shifted and squeaked, nuzzling closer to each other, too young to open their bulging eyes to the sunlight.

While I and the rest of the world waited restlessly for things to change—for the better or for worse—the chicks grew a little each day, oblivious to my angst. The tree blossomed around them, sheltering the nest in a canopy of vibrant pink.

One day, I peeked into the nest to find four sets of watchful, jet eyes peering back at me. From then on, the chicks were quiet and still whenever I visited, but life radiated from their tiny bodies. They flourished, contentedly nestled in each other's company, peaceful in the care of their attentive parents. To me, they were a promise that the chaos of the human world wasn't all-consuming. As pandemic restrictions stretched on, my personal world had shrunk to my neighborhood, my street, my yard, my house. But the little ones got steadily closer to being ready to explore the wider world.

It wasn't long before the hatchlings barely fit in the nest, jumbled in an awkward pile of brown feathers and hungry yellow beaks. Within only a couple weeks, they had outgrown their nursery, and I found the nest empty for the first time. I knew it would happen eventually, but I was still disappointed at how soon the birds had left me behind.

Time kept passing: The spring days slipped away even as the individual hours crawled. The pandemic and its fallout worsened while my life felt stagnant. I often found myself staring out of the window at the trees in our backyard, watching the chickadees, phoebes, finches, and starlings flutter in and out of view.

I wondered about my chicks each time I spotted a juvenile robin with its telltale speckled breast. Where were they? Were they okay, out in the big, dangerous world with nothing but their three-ounce mother to guide and protect them?

Many of those weeks are a blur in my memory. I don't remember many details about how I spent my time, only that I was constantly worried about my loved ones and wondering if life would ever go back to the way it was before.

The blossoms fell from the crabapple tree, dusting the ground with petals like pink confetti, and were replaced with thousands of dark green leaves. Robins and other birds stopped by for a quick rest from time to time, but they always flew off if I got too close. Sometimes they poked around in the lawn, hunting for bugs, scurrying over the grass and under the tall maple tree on the other side of the driveway.

Then, one day, something dramatic happened. It started with a strange sound, sudden and raucous, that I could hear from inside the house. It reminded me of a flock of birds—very upset birds—and it didn't end; instead of a brief alarm call signaling a swift flight, the commotion carried on, filled with urgency. I'd never heard anything quite like it, so I hurried to the window and tried to make sense of the action playing out in front of me.

A hawk was on the lawn under the maple tree. And it wasn't alone: It was facing off with a little group of robins. In shocked fascination, I watched as they squawked at the hawk with the fierceness of a battle cry. They darted back and forth in a flurry of flapping wings, advancing and retreating, charging and feinting. The hawk watched them warily, its wings half furled, like it was unsure how to handle the tiny squadron.

The brave little birds were mottle-breasted juveniles, and they looked so small beside the hawk. Could these be my chicks? And were they really taking on a predator more than twice their size?

An adult robin—larger than the fledglings, with a bold, rusty breast and dark head—appeared suddenly from above. It did a kamikaze dive, barreling straight into the hawk's back. The hawk barely flinched, but the mother robin didn't give up. It pulled back a bit before speeding in for another blow, and another.

It was then that I realized there was one more robin I hadn't seen, another fledgling—and it was pinned beneath the hawk's taloned foot.

I don't usually begrudge a bird of prey for feeding itself, even at the expense of another animal's life. But that day, I couldn't bear to watch it kill the helpless little robin.

"Hey!" I shouted, tapping on the window, a rush of adrenaline making me consider running outside to intervene.

The hawk clocked me with its keen eye, and it must have decided I was scarier than it was hungry. With a few flaps of its wings, it was gone. The robins scattered as well—startled by me or the hawk's sudden flight, I don't know. But they didn't go far, sheltering in the branches of the maple tree or underneath the nearby bushes. Because the hawk hadn't taken its catch with it. One robin remained in the grass.

The unfortunate bird lay where the hawk had abandoned it, and I held my breath as I stared. Was the poor thing dead? I would be devastated to see one of my chicks with its life cut so short.

I had only a moment to wonder before the little body stirred. It managed to get itself upright, crouching in the grass with its head twitching side to side, scanning its surroundings. I was amazed that it didn't even look injured, just a little stunned. I wondered if it was just as surprised as I was that it was unscathed.

Gathering its wits, the little survivor hopped to its feet and darted under a bush to join its siblings. Satisfied that it was safe if the hawk tried to recover its lunch, I sat down in the nearest chair and found myself laughing with disbelief. I'd never seen such animal drama outside of a documentary.

It's possible that the little band of birdy warriors wasn't the same chicks I had watched grow up, but I felt that it was. And I was so proud of them! If the family hadn't confronted the hawk, I doubt the hawk would have hesitated to start tearing its victim to pieces. And I certainly wouldn't have come running to scare it off.

I know the hawk was only one of many daily challenges my chicks would face their first spring and beyond. The world can be cruel and deadly for a small creature in so many ways, just as it can feel uncaring and dangerous to me. But that day, I realized the little birds were resilient and fiercer in the face of those challenges than I'd expected.

To this day, when I see a robin in my yard, I wonder if it's one of my chicks, migrating back to the place it was born. I'll never know what happened to them after the hawk attack, but every year at the first hint of spring, robins start to appear in our yard. They build nests, find mates, and feed and watch over their young. I can usually spot a nest in one of our trees or under our deck. Some years, there's even one in the same crook of the crabapple tree.

Before 2020, I never paid much attention to robins. They're common birds here—nothing special or exciting, I'd thought. But now, that ubiquitousness is something I love about them. In the warmer months, I see them everywhere, every day, and hear their familiar songs. And I think about the chicks that reminded me to hope again.

five

Morning Meetings, Evening Prayers

ANDREA DOERING

It was one of those mornings when you wake feeling like you've never slept. The past and the future pressed into my dreams, and they didn't have anything good to say. As I started to wake up, of course, the present needs also clamored for some attention. This didn't bode well for the day ahead.

The saving grace was it was one of the first mild days of spring, where the air promises that more warmth is on the way, and the wind is light and friendly. Which meant I could take my morning walk along the boardwalk that runs along a small section of our village beach, looking out on Long Island Sound. No matter what, a morning walk always clears my head and brings my attention up out of whatever is on the list for the day. But walking along the water is my favorite walk. The waves, the water, and the open space are a gift on any day—but particularly on days like this.

That morning I didn't wait. Before breakfast, before anyone could talk to me and add to my list of things to do, I walked down my street toward the water. When I reached it, I smiled. Everything was as I hoped. A light breeze from the west, the sun shining, the winter sticks bobbing on the tide, placeholders for their summer replacements of boat moorings.

But what I had forgotten was that though my day was just beginning, the seabirds were already making their plans. Out in our small harbor, a few work floats—flat docks, anchored to the harbor floor—had been recast as the cormorant boardroom. A flight of cormorants, dark bodies with a flat gloss that reflected every bit of light coming from the water, huddled at one end, tipping it slightly off center. I couldn't help but look at that grouping and imagine what they were communicating to each other. How would a flight of cormorants start their workday? Do they talk over the flight conditions, communicating in their own way the wind speed and direction and setting out a flight plan? Do they review yesterday's catch and share areas of the Sound where the fishing was fine? Perhaps they have a mental map of the harbor and divide up the "work" into sections? It so resembled a morning meeting that I had to laugh. But I also started to feel lighter, my burdens not so heavy.

The gulls seemed like they'd been up since dawn—they were already in the air, diving for mussels, dropping them on the rock seawall right below me. Gulls are quick—they have to be. Their now-broken mussel won't be there long, and I watched as the gulls wheeled quickly around to land and eat before another of the flock could grab it. Perhaps they also have a morning meeting, but by the time I see them, it's all action.

This morning's walk then gave the best bird gift—my favorite, one who is not always present, the lone blue heron. He was perched on the rock breakwater, not more than fifty feet from where the boardwalk ends. I don't know if it's a male or a female, but I think of it as a male. He was so still. The wind ruffled his top crest, and if I hadn't slowed down to watch the other birds, I would have easily missed him. Behind him, the gray rocks and blue water just about masked his existence. But there he was, preparing for the day. The antithesis of the constant activity of the gulls was watching and waiting. The wind picked up a bit, but that attentive, still figure would move at a signal known only to him. And as I waited and watched with him, I experienced a moment when time doesn't seem to exist, and the past and the future go back to their respective spots. Suddenly there was a great burst into flight. His neck stretched, his wings opened, and he had an almost vertical launch, quickly tucking in his feet and neck, now a beautiful, streamlined vessel, gliding low over the shoreline. He made one pass along the beach. He'd found what he seemed to know would be there, and with a quick dive, he was up with a fish and heading to the beach.

Watching the birds start their morning before I started mine, in their own unique ways, was a great reminder to me to consider my day differently and not to dread the tasks. The birds reminded me my day doesn't always have to look the same. Sometimes I need a morning huddle. Sometimes I just need to get up and get started, like the gulls. The heron reminded me that activity is not always visible. The thinking, the planning, and the learning—they don't look like much to the observer. But they have their place and also yield results. And all of it reminded me of a favorite quote by Robert Capon in *The Supper of the Lamb*: "When we go to work, we go forth, by obedience to vocation, to draw the world into the Passion."[1]

The end of the day found me back at the beach. The days were now longer, and that mild weather had graced the entire day. This time I took in the full scene at the harbor, looking for my working friends. The heron was gone, nesting in some hidden place. The gulls were tucked into small bundles on the beach, finally still, each pointed toward the wind. New to the landscape was the flock of mallard ducks I knew spent their days in the marsh across the harbor; now it was their time to come back further into the harbor for the night, swimming single file across the water.

And the cormorants? The cormorants had abandoned the dock. Those I could see this evening were perched on posts of decayed pilings, wings wide to the setting sun, drying their feathers the way a fisherman dries his nets. I spent some time watching them, again trying to imagine their life. What I saw, and what stayed with me, was that the day's work was done. They were at peace; they had been given their daily fish or eel. Their posture reminded me of one of the most natural poses for worship—standing with arms wide, open to the heavens, open to God's next move in the world.

I don't know all the habits of these birds. But I do know what I saw at the end of the day—they're not working. For the seabirds, everything changes at the end of the day. And the same can be true for me.

My day can have a beginning and end. The truth is that I, too, have finished the work for the day. It doesn't have to spill over into my dreams, and into all hours. I, too, have been given my daily bread. Though I don't always throw my arms wide at the end of the day, perhaps I should. It's a great move that can open me up to the next great move of God.

six

Out of the Blue

DeVONNA R. ALLISON

I shuffled my way to the kitchen and switched on the coffeepot. Most mornings I hit the ground running, but today I had a little rare free time, and I enjoyed the quiet. A slight rustling sound from the corner of our dining room interrupted my reverie. A smile crept across my face, and I crossed the room to lift the flowered cloth from the birdcage.

"JoJo!" The bright green and yellow parakeet spoke his own name in raspy greeting.

"Well, hello, Jo . . . whaddya know?" I teased him.

Ruffling and preening, the little bird purred softly, cocked his head as if to see me better with his bright black eye, and let loose a stream of friendly chirps and tweets. Hopping from perch to swing, JoJo reached up and rang the tiny bell suspended from the top of his cage, and I couldn't help but chuckle.

"You little show-off!"

Living in the country, our family has often been the recipient of "castoff" pets. Among these pets were pregnant mama cats, heavy with young, and, surprisingly, chickens. The chickens' former owners, mostly backyard hobbyists, had their egg-filled dreams squashed when their spring chicks turned into early-summer roosters. We took in a pony destined for the slaughterhouse and a feisty Manchester terrier who found his way to our home. The terrier, Ivan, was labeled "destructive" by his owners, but it turns out the dog was just anxious and frustrated at being caged thirteen hours a day while his owners worked. There were no more cages for Ivan at our house and never any destructive behavior.

We even "found" a mini pig who wandered down our six-hundred-foot driveway one day. We heard an earth-shattering uproar out in the yard and found Gypsy, as we named the pig, running and squalling for her life, being chased by our pony, Poker, round and round Poker's pen. Gypsy had gone under the gate to eat Poker's grain, but Poker wasn't sharing. He went after the uninvited pig with teeth bared and squeals of outrage! We rescued Gypsy (quite literally) from the pony, and once I'd caught my breath, I figured she was probably an "impulse buy" from the local flea market. People forget when making these purchases that an adorable little three-pound piglet grows into a forty-five-pound adolescent with a big appetite and a strong desire to root up your garden.

Sadly, some of these pets, like Gypsy, were unceremoniously dumped in our woods. Others, like Ivan and Poker, came to us because word got around that we took in strays and rejects. Occasionally we *did* turn down an animal, as in the case of the "tame skunk," but for the most part we were up for a challenge. If we couldn't keep the animal long-term, we would find them a good home with someone else.

While Ivan became our young son's constant companion, both in the house and out, most of our adoptees lived outside.

We had a nice setup on our twelve acres. There was a sturdy divided chicken coop, a pig run, separate goat and pony pens, and a small barn where we housed our orphans. But JoJo, he moved right into our home.

I worked as the secretary of a small rural church. Once a month the older women of the church held a quilting bee in the fellowship hall. They always invited me to join them for their hot lunches. One bright fall day, while filling my plate with salads and casserole, I overheard a conversation at the table.

"I was cleaning out my flower beds when I felt a little something land on my back. I thought a leaf had fallen off the tree," Edith said. "I turned my head to brush it off, and there sat a pretty little parakeet!"

The other ladies oohed.

"I offered him my finger, and he jumped right on!" Edith said.

She carried the little bird inside. Edith and her husband, Robert, kept a canary, so they offered the little stranger a dish of birdseed and some water, which he attacked greedily.

While Edith and Robert were amazed and delighted to have found the wandering parakeet, their canary, Peter, was not a fan. Peter scolded and fluttered angrily around his cage at the sight of the parakeet. Robert moved the new bird to another room where Peter couldn't see him, but whenever Peter heard the parakeet chirp, he screamed in response.

Robert put up signs, hoping they could return the friendly bird to its owner.

Edith shook her head. "No one has claimed the parakeet, and we just can't keep him. We're afraid Peter will hurt him, and Peter has stopped singing." Edith sighed. The other women murmured in sympathy.

I had a forkful of casserole halfway to my mouth when I became aware that conversation at the table had ceased and all eyes were turned on me. I put my fork down, wiped my mouth with a napkin, and turned to Edith.

"So . . . does the cage come with him?" I asked.

The day after Robert and Edith dropped the parakeet off at our house, Peter began singing his heart out again.

I hadn't kept a parakeet since I was a little girl. I'd had a pale blue beauty named Joey. From that experience I knew this new bird was a male because of the bright blue cere band across the bridge of his bill. I named this new parakeet JoJo in memory of that long-ago pet.

JoJo huddled quietly at the back of his cage when he first arrived. Our whole family admired him—he was a real beauty, bright green and vivid yellow. After several weeks he grew accustomed to the sights and sounds of our busy home. Our three children, the two dogs, and our one indoor cat all watched JoJo and in turn were studied by him. It didn't take long for everyone to get used to each other, and JoJo was chirping happily.

JoJo quickly got used to his name, and I was delighted to hear him repeat it after a few months! In winter I put his cage near the window so he could watch wild birds at the feeders, and in the warmer spring and summer months, I put his cage out on the front porch where he sang and preened in the mild Michigan sunshine.

One morning, after I'd put JoJo's cage out in the morning sun, I heard him shrieking in alarm. I ran to the porch and found one of our adopted kittens sitting on top of JoJo's cage! The kitten was just curious, for now, but I knew I had to take precautions. I shooed the kitten away and asked my husband, Earl, to install a hook so I could hang JoJo's cage from the front porch where he could enjoy fresh air in peace and safety. We even saw hummingbirds buzzing around JoJo once in a while, checking him out.

Though JoJo came to us during a busy time in our lives, he endeared himself to us. He was a little bird with tons of personality! He shrieked excitedly whenever our phone rang, and when he heard birds on television, JoJo sang and chirped to them. He treated us like we were part of his flock. JoJo greeted us enthusiastically when we returned home, and every time we gathered at the table, he would hop down to his bowl and eat along with us.

Some of my favorite times with JoJo were when I talked to him, telling him what a good boy he was and how very beautiful he was, and he would sit and slowly close his eyes halfway. Basking in the sound of my voice, JoJo was the picture of bliss and purred softly back.

I still think of JoJo, all these years later, when I hear birds chirping on television or see parakeets for sale at the flea market. He remains one of my favorite rescues, the little bird who dropped out of the sky and into our hearts.

seven

My Feathered Friends

KAREN FOSTER

My feathered friends and I have a gentlewoman's agreement. They reside in my five-acre woods, build their nests along my porch rafters, gorge on a smorgasbord of store-bought sunflower seeds, bathe in my birdbaths, trawl my lawn for worms, and consume nectar from my garden flowers. All this—free of charge.

Somebody has to pay, though. That's where I come in. Year round, I buy the seeds, sweep the bird droppings off my porch, fill the birdbaths with fresh water, care for the lawn, and prune the flowers.

But my relentless job is refilling my hummingbird feeder with sugar water so the world's tiniest bird can guzzle nectar like it's an all-you-can-eat buffet. Seriously! How can a bird that weighs less than a dime drink so much sugar water? We should all be so lucky.

My glass hummingbird feeder hangs from the roof's edge of my front porch. I rarely need look at the feeder to see if it's empty because my hummingbirds let me know when I'm shirking my job.

Just last week, I stood at my kitchen sink, holding a cup of hot Earl Grey tea when a hummingbird dashed to the windowpane and hovered at eye level. What a handsome little fellow with his emerald back and crown gleaming beneath the morning sun. Compared to that of the less-colorful female hummingbirds, his iridescent red throat identified him as a male. He cocked his head and drew closer as though admiring his reflection in the window.

"Yes, you're gorgeous," I said. But then I noticed the thin vase on my windowsill, which held a red carnation. "Are you admiring yourself? Or my flower?"

I don't know if this bird read lips, but he zoomed toward my front porch. I leaned over the sink and watched him plunge his long bill into one of the holes in my hummingbird feeder's red base. Then he darted away without satisfying his hunger.

"Sorry," I moaned, setting my teacup on the counter. "I didn't know it was empty."

Perhaps it's the mother hen in me who looks after my household before feeding myself, but a sense of urgency took over. Whatever I'd written at the top of my to-do list that morning became number two. Feeding the hummingbirds became my priority.

I measured the ingredients of my homemade nectar into an aluminum pan. Four cups of water and a cup of sugar. Then I turned on the stove burner and waited for the water to get hot enough to dissolve the sugar. Once that happened, I set aside the pan and allowed the water to cool before I poured it into the feeder. Didn't want the hummingbirds to burn their tongues.

I went outside to fetch the feeder and spied Mr. Hummingbird perched on a limb like he owned the world. His small stature belied his power. After all, he'd strong-armed this sixtysomething woman to resupply his hummingbird food before I'd finished my tea. I could almost read his thoughts as he studied me. *About time, lady.*

Standing on my tiptoes, I leaned over the wooden porch rail and struggled to remove the feeder that hung from a nail. Did I mention my porch stands eight feet above the ground? As I glanced down at our concrete walkway, I almost lost my balance and wondered, *Who's the bird brain in this scenario?*

Maybe I wasn't moving fast enough, because I heard high-pitched squeaks and the whirr of wings as Mr. Hummingbird brushed past me. Then he dive-bombed the feeder clutched in my hand.

"What are you doing?" I fussed, waving him away. "Are you nuts? Why would you attack the hand that feeds you?"

He flew backward a few inches (a feat only hummingbirds can do) and looked me in the eye. Hummingbirds are territorial, and maybe he felt impatient, but getting in my face wasn't going to make me move any faster. I pointed to the tree. "Take a breather!"

To my surprise, he flew back to his limb. And I returned to the kitchen for the nasty part of my job—cleaning the feeder. Pesky ants invariably follow their sweet tooth into the feeder's holes and drown. That day was no exception. A mound of dead, wet ants fell from their watery grave and into the sink when I removed the base.

Uhhh! I wrinkled my nose in disgust, rinsed the ants into the drain stopper, and tossed them into the garbage can. My cup of tea stood next to the sink, cool to the touch. But unlike the hummingbirds, I'd lost my appetite.

Sugar water dripped on my pinewood floor as I carried the feeder toward the front door, leaving a sticky trail. *Add mopping to my list,* I told myself. But what awaited me erased those thoughts. My feathered friend must have spread the word. "Breakfast is served!" For not one but five hummingbirds were suspended in the air, lined up like incoming helicopters waiting their turn to land.

I listened to the hum of their wings beating the air while I carefully placed the feeder on the nail. Mission accomplished. I stepped back, eager to watch them feast. But one of the hummingbirds flew out of line and dove toward my forehead like an incoming missile. I squeezed my eyes shut and turned my head, waiting for impact. Thankfully, goosebumps pricked my flesh instead of his sharp bill. Duly warned, I moved further back.

Or maybe, I laughed to myself, that bird intended to peck me on the forehead with a kiss.

I knew his intentions weren't sentimental when he shoved himself in front of the other birds and took the first drink. When he flew off, a flurry of hummingbirds surrounded the feeder. A few of them waited for their turns. Others landed on the base and took their sweet time to eat. Some returned for a second helping. The smaller birds hesitated when they saw me and darted away without eating. So I stood behind my screen door and grinned while I watched them dine as though I'd served filet mignon instead of sugar water.

What can I say? My hummingbirds expect no less from me. They act entitled. And yet, I never get a word of thanks. I expect that's how God feels toward me when I fail to thank him for my daily bread and blessings.

I mentioned earlier that my feathered friends and I have an agreement. They live here and feast for free. And I try to meet their needs. But I do get something from my efforts. My yard has become an outdoor aviary. Hummingbirds aren't the only birds that call this place home. Woodpeckers, red-tailed hawks, yellow finches, blackbirds, sparrows, blue jays, and robins have all taken up residence; my oaks and pines are filled with birdsong and endless activity.

It brings me great joy when I find feathers on the ground. Each feather is unique in length, texture, and color. The smallest one is gray-white like the underpart of a hummingbird. Whenever I look at these feathers, I think of my beloved birds. And they remind me that God loves me even more.

eight

Mr. Bird

JANE GWALTNEY

In the summer of 1979, our family received an unexpected addition. Just what a mother of a toddler needs, right?

I wasn't prepared for a tiny, naked, squirming blob whose open mouth was half the size of its body. A newly hatched orphaned sparrow is anything but shy. FEED ME!

First things first. A box of tissues served as a warm, comfy, easy-to-clean nest. FEED ME!

What a dilemma. I manufactured breast milk for my human baby boy but wasn't equipped to nourish a demanding avian. Phone calls to local wildlife rehabs yielded a grim reality. Sparrows didn't qualify. They were and still are considered invasive pests, unprotected by laws. The upside: They can be legally housed as pets. These days, Facebook groups offer fact-based advice for house sparrow parents. Some rehabs have even changed their policies and will accept sparrows if not overwhelmed by songbirds and native species.

A wildlife volunteer kindly gave me detailed instructions on what and how to feed my helpless critter. Pitiful peeps from the tissue box next to my bed woke me about twenty minutes apart, and a long scrawny neck topped with a marble-sized head popped up. That huge gaping beak knew me personally now: FEED ME, MAMA! I dropped in moistened kitten chow each time he begged, until his crop filled and slumber overtook. I had experienced sleep deprivation with my human newborn, but it paled in comparison to this ordeal. My respect and awe for the dedication of wildlife parents reached "limitless."

Intervals between feedings quickly and mercifully increased. Eyes opened. Was the comical creature sporting pin feathers and downy fuzz on the cranium a boy or girl? I named him Mr. Bird. If need be, Ms. Bird was a future option.

Meanwhile, Mr. Bird's transformation was in overdrive. He soon slept full nights, made clumsy attempts to groom itchy pin feathers . . . and stood up for two whole seconds at a time on those spindly legs. I fastened a perch to the box, and he clutched it and my fingers, fighting to stay on. In a matter of days, pin feather sheaths were shredded by his beak, and his first coat of juvenile feathers began to appear. He jumped for joy, right onto Mama's hand. Time to abandon the box and explore!

A safe cage, fitted with perches and ladders, was his gymnasium with a view. His fully formed beak was his new instrument to satisfy curiosity. His entire world was ripe for the pleasure of pecking. He pecked at anything and everything, especially the seeds on the floor of the cage and in Mama's hands. And wings were definitely for flapping. He wasn't sure why just yet . . .

I was amused to watch Mr. Bird take in his surroundings. Who was that fascinating little human? He monopolized Mama's attention, made funny noises, and flew low around the house.

It was time to formally introduce my babies to each other. My son, Gabe, was gentle with animals. Our corgi mix, Pee-wee, a family addition from my 1970 job at the Humane Society, was his closest pal. Gabe's eyes grew wide as I let Mr. Bird inspect his hand. "He tickles!" A friendship was sealed.

The four-legged furry thing that kept zipping through the room would be dealt with . . . later.

At this stage, Mr. Bird's instincts urged him to use his wings to take to the air. I pondered how this would happen without support from his avian mama. Sparrows landed on the windowsill to initiate staring matches. Jumping and flapping when they flew off, Mr. Bird would go splat on his stubby tail. He needed no coaxing to settle into the warm comfort of my cupped hands and reply to my "mama's brave boy" with cluck-cluck sounds . . .

Soon, his flight feathers lengthened. He learned to grip perches and fingers and flap vigorously. He would tighten his grip, stretch his legs . . . lifting upward, chirping with glee. That first sunny day his feet let go, he sailed and landed—a bit lopsided—on top of his cage. Cheers! My fledgling was a flight-school graduate. No stopping him now.

Behold the first big molt! Mr. Bird emerged as a cranky teenager, ridding himself of all remaining baby feathers in a frenzied hurry. He pecked viciously at the disheveled reflection in his mirror.

As usual, his safe place was on my shoulder, snuggled against the pulse in my neck. When we both needed solace from a challenging day, we napped together on the couch. His coveted spot was on my chest, directly over my heart.

Glossy feathers replaced the dull frazzled ones at an amazing rate, revealing Mr. Bird as a male. He preened constantly, his long silvery tail contrasting with patterned splashes of rust brown, black, and white. My adult sparrow was gorgeous.

He agreed, parading his handsome self in front of every reflective surface. His flights were lightning strikes. A fly or spider on the wall didn't stand a chance. Gabe and I gradually stopped looking away as the snacks were devoured but politely declined when Mr. Bird offered to share. We weren't as generous when he started landing knee-deep in our dinner plates. He was sentenced to a time-out in his cage to sulk. An intelligent problem solver, he employed a new tactic: patiently sitting beside our plates, guilting us with his eyes. It worked. He was awarded sparrow-sized nibbles on his own Bert and Ernie plate.

That's when a lurker from the shadows found her voice. "Woof!" Pee-wee poked her head from beneath a footstool, then scurried from the room to escape a dive-bombing by Mr. Bird. My heart sank. We'd forgotten Pee-wee's established treat-eating ritual at dinnertime.

Peaceful coexistence was an absolute goal. My son and I shared a house with my parents. Over the years, work schedules and a series of hamsters, guinea pigs, goldfish, and a bunny named Freddy would all test that goal . . .

Mr. Bird adapted, in his own sassy way, to our multigeneration/multispecies family. It was a balancing act built on a foundation of mutual love and respect.

Pee-wee admired the winged avenger at a safe distance and even shared her toys and her pal, Gabe, reluctantly or not. When the canine beast was reprimanded for overzealous barking with "Shut up, Pee-wee," we were astonished to one day hear Mr. Bird's squeaky echo. That, and humorous imitations of my sneezes, were preserved on my father's cassette recordings.

My most bizarre memory is of Mr. Bird snatching a contact lens off my eye and playing catch-me-if-you-can as I chased him. I panicked as he lingered on top of a doorframe, spinning the lens in his beak. With great effort, I composed myself, held out my hand, and asked him to return it. Immediately, he flew down and placed it in my palm.

An urgent trip to my optometrist's office showed no damage to my eye or the lens. I doubt the doctor believed my explanation for the visit. His parting summation was "Never heard that one before."

Mr. Bird's mischief entertained us all. One of his favorite games was hiding, silent, in odd places and then popping out at us. And I did find it relaxing when he obsessively groomed all around my fingernails. During my bird research I discovered this area commonly hosts mites, invisible to the human eye. Birds can see them and regard them as yummy. I appreciated the manicures.

It goes without saying, but I'll say it anyway. The beautiful bond of trust and love I experienced with this complex avian, this gift from the Creator, was one of the most profound of my life. I'm forever grateful for the lessons this lowly human learned.

This brings me to my final memory, in 1989 . . .

Ten years. Gabe and Mr. Bird had matured together, but Gabe was still a child. Mr. Bird had lived more than three times his "sparrow in the wild" average lifespan of three years. Our feisty little warrior was beginning to slow down.

Birds are experts at disguising signs of aging and illness. Their instincts are to fool predators. Mr. Bird wasn't fooling Mama. His naps increased and he regressed to baby bird cuddling. His appetite decreased and he allowed me to hand feed him flies he'd snapped at and missed.

Pee-wee, age seven when Gabe was born, had died, and the trail of grief was still fresh. I knew Mr. Bird was glimpsing the panoramic watercolor wash of colors in the sky, far away . . . and I knew Gabe was unaware. A local veterinarian had given me a bottle of antibiotics. Gabe was sure Mr. Bird would be fine. I wasn't ready to destroy that hope. I hid my tears, as if I too were a sparrow in disguise, hiding from Death the predator.

A week later, I could hide no more. Before I got into bed that night, I put Mr. Bird's cage nearby, door open. He flew the short distance from his sleep perch to my bed—landing on my chest, over my heart. My baby's eyes were as bright as ever, but his feathers were fluffed to preserve body heat. I cupped my hands, and he hopped inside, clucking softly.

I was shocked by the coolness of his belly against my skin. He shivered. His eyes seemed to me to beg not for food, but love . . . and release.

I don't remember how long our eyes were locked, or how many kisses I put on his head before I said what he needed to hear. "I love you, my sweet baby. I always will. It's all right. You can go now."

His eyes closed.

The following afternoon, after school, I took my son in my arms. He cried, with a raw grief I'd never heard before. So did Mama.

nine

Magical Mergansers

THOMAS KIENZLE

My wife, Debra, and I enjoy being out in nature, especially when we can take binoculars, cameras, and long lenses along. We particularly like to photograph birds since they are so numerous, all different sizes, and so colorful. An area we've discovered that has many species of birds is along the Gulf Coast of Alabama, from Orange Beach, Gulf Shores, Fort Morgan, and over to Dauphin Island. In fact, the ferry ride over to Dauphin Island can yield surprising pelagic birds, such as gannets, which we've seen several times on our adventures to this area of Alabama.

Many times on our way to hiking trails or the ferry to Dauphin Island, I noticed the sign for Jeff Friend Trail but never said anything about stopping and checking it out. So one night at dinner I suggested we stop and investigate this trail first thing in the morning, especially since it was close to the water. We knew from experience there is always wildlife by water, be it birds, butterflies, beasts, or all of the above.

Next morning was one of those perfect starts to the day with crisp, cool, but still air, and the sun was just beginning to make an appearance. When we pulled in, I was pleased to note that when the trail left the parking lot, it immediately headed away from the main road and toward Little Lagoon, which is adjacent to parts of the one-mile-loop Jeff Friend Trail. I hoped that we would be able to walk far enough away to lose all sound of cars so we could enjoy the quiet solitude of being in the woods and by water. With binoculars and cameras around our necks, we found a small sandy trail by the water that was less than two feet wide. But it was plenty wide enough for us to walk single file. We soon saw several bluebirds, with one posing on top of a tall snag. With a blue sky as background, it was a photo op that I could not pass up.

A few minutes later, we spotted what appeared to be an osprey nest fifty yards away and what could only be a silhouette of the head of an owl sticking up. This was no surprise to us, as some owls are known to use previously occupied nests. The distinctive horned "ears" could not be mistaken for anything except a great horned owl. Yet another photo op even though we weren't as close as I would have liked. As we moved past, we noted the owl watching us. Maybe she was curious as to why there were humans disturbing her so early in the morning.

As we walked along, I noticed that the trees on one side of the trail muted the traffic noise from the main road. It wasn't the complete solitude I was looking for, but that was okay since we were out in nature and enjoying ourselves. At the farthest point of the trail, I suggested we go off-trail and walk along the water toward Childress Point, which extends out into the lagoon a short ways. I was hoping to see something interesting on the water. In particular, I wanted to spot a common loon or even some bufflehead ducks, which are birds we don't see too often in our home in western Tennessee.

As we looked out over the lagoon, a movement in the corner of my eye caught my attention. "Look," I whispered to my wife. As if by magic, a spectacular sight appeared before our eyes. More than twenty common mergansers were in a feeding frenzy right in front of us and only a few yards from shore. (Mergansers are a type of diving duck that inhabit lakes and streams and like to feed on fish, although not exclusively.) They moved from left to right in the calm water and caused almost no disturbance on the surface when they dove under. They were sliding quietly below the surface while others were popping up and then immediately diving again. They dove into their prey again and again as they moved past us, the red and green heads of the females and males standing out in the early morning sunlight.

Snapping out of my trance, I quickly brought my camera up and took a few photos, but I was too late. This photo op had already moved on. But that didn't matter to me. It didn't matter that I had not captured a prize image that we could hang on the wall. It didn't matter that we never got to see exactly what type of fish they were feeding on. What did matter was that we had witnessed something special, something we had never seen before.

I didn't realize just how special watching the mergansers had been until we turned around and started back to our car. Everything stressful, such as my job, rush hour traffic, bills to pay, etc., had been forgotten. I was so absorbed in watching them that I was one with nature—nothing else existed except for the feeding mergansers, and for those few minutes, life was as it was meant to be: camera in hand and sharing the outdoors with my wife.

But now I could again hear the cars on the main road. A car door slammed as more people arrived at the parking lot. Adults talking, children giggling. I couldn't help but feel bad for the newcomers. I felt like shouting to them, "You missed it!" But I held my tongue and only nodded an acknowledgment as we made space for them to pass us on the small sandy trail.

What an incredible experience it was to have been mesmerized by Mother Nature, even if only for a few moments. But those few moments with the mergansers were enough.

ten

Hello! Hello! Hello!

CHRISSY DRZEWIECKI

I was ten years old when my Uncle Al passed away. My Aunt Mary was devasted and beyond consoling, and her sidekick poodle, Timmy, became her whole world. When Timmy died, Aunt Mary became depressed after losing both him and her first and only love of her life.

Aunt Mary was tough as nails, but these losses hit her to the core of her being. She continued working at Macy's in New York City, which kept her busy and out of the empty Brooklyn apartment where memories crushed her spirit.

But she needed a companion. What pet could she possibly get that wouldn't require taking the three-story trip up and down those stairs several times a day, as she did with Timmy? No matter the weather, it was what she'd had to do. In the summer, there was no air-conditioning, only fans. And there were no elevators back in the 1940s. The winter months were brutal, but she never complained.

Sitting in her recliner one Saturday afternoon, a book in hand, she had an aha moment. She hopped on the subway, got off at the next stop, and walked into a downtown Brooklyn pet store. Wandering around in a daze, not quite knowing what she was looking for, she eventually noticed that a bright blue bird, with black feathered wings and tail tips, seemed to be squawking at her. She'd never owned a bird before. She kept walking. It kept squawking. Louder. She went back and stood in front of the cage. There were at least four other parakeets in it, and they were quiet. Not this one. It kept coming toward her, hanging on the wired side of the cage, head cocking side to side. She was convinced he wanted to go home with her.

Thankfully, parakeets are a small- to medium-sized species of parrot with long tail feathers. She could handle small.

Blue parakeets are also known as budgies and are native to Australia. They are clean freaks, and their cages must be cleaned several times a week. This worked out well, as my Aunt Mary was a meticulous housekeeper. When we visited her in the summer, I was always afraid to sit on her couch. Most times I'd be on Daddy's lap. There was absolutely nothing for a young child to do in that apartment except get yelled at.

The first time I saw Skippy, we'd walked into her apartment and a gruff voice said, "Hello, hello, hello," over and over. That was my introduction to a house bird. *Annoying,* I thought. But the cage had a cloth cover over it. My aunt removed it, and I could barely see inside the cage, even when on my tippy-toes. "Hello," it said again. Daddy lifted me up. "Hello," I said in my soft, shy voice.

When we would visit, Aunt Mary would quiz me on my knowledge of parakeets, though all I wanted was to hear Skippy talk. The only facts I recalled were if it had stripes from the base of the beak to the top of its head, it was three to four months old. And if the skin above its beak was solid blue or violet, it was a male. Plain white meant it was a female. Aunt Mary had made me aware of that fact right quick, as the bird was so pretty, I mistakenly thought it must be a girl. Plus, Skippy kept yelling, "Pretty bird, pretty bird," at the mirror my aunt hung in the cage. She said it kept him busy.

I fell in love with that bird, and of course I wanted one of my own. But to my chagrin, Daddy said no. Begging would not help. I had to be satisfied spending time with Skippy during those visits. He began to trust me and allowed me to stick my finger in his cage to land on. He'd play a little game; he'd back up on his perch, then move closer, then back up again until he finally skipped onto my little finger. It sure was a funny feeling that first time. He'd wrap his little digits around my fingers, and I'd gently pull him through the cage door, and then he'd instantly fly onto my shoulder. He'd learned the word *kisses*, and he'd peck the tip of my little nose, causing a giggle. And oh, how soft his little head was. I had to be reminded to pet him gently.

After many decades of living in that old apartment in Brooklyn, Aunt Mary followed my mom and dad to the sunshine state of Florida. Skippy's cage was situated in the screened-in sunroom. It appeared he was a happy, pretty bird. I could see he was getting a bit older, as his eyes were no longer black but instead were light gray, and he became less active when we visited. This made me sad, not for me but for my Aunt Mary.

Living in Florida made it easier on my Aunt Mary's bad legs. She continued riding her three-wheel bicycle, and Skippy would always greet her upon her return with a haughty, "Hello, hello, hello." Which she'd do in turn right back at him.

Thank goodness Skippy was well trained and stayed inside the house when not in his cage. He never tried flying out the open door. If he had, he might have joined the wild parakeets, which lined the wires from one end of the city to the next. And all were budgies. It was mesmerizing to me. Wild parakeets! I've never seen anything like it again.

I don't remember when Aunt Mary lost Skippy, but I do recall she was sad. And I wanted to keep Skippy's memory alive and get one just like him. Once again, it was a big fat no from Daddy. *Maybe,* I thought, *when I'm older I shall.*

eleven

Tah-Kah,
Our Rescued Crow

MARY BETH LAUFER

The year I turned twelve, my brother had a pet crow. The bird came to live with us in the spring and left in the fall, and for that short time he was a member of our family. I didn't realize how unusual this was until I grew up. Now I look back with fond memories.

We kids knew it was wrong to remove a bird from its nest, and my brother Gerry wouldn't have done it without a good reason. He was exploring the woods one day and came across dead baby crows beneath a pine tree. He looked up and spotted a nest high above him. Had these baby birds fallen to their deaths after their parents failed to return?

Gerry thought there might be other baby crows up there, still alive, that would surely die if he didn't rescue them. He overcame his fear of heights long enough to shimmy up the tall tree. A single crow remained in the nest. The tiny bird opened its beak and squawked. Gerry carefully placed it in his pocket and climbed down.

He kept the crow in a cardboard box on the radiator in his bedroom to keep it warm. My younger sisters and I stared in awe at the little ball of black fluff.

"I'm calling him Tah-Kah," Gerry said. The name was similar to the noise the bird made.

Its beak opened wide. "What are you going to feed him?" I asked.

Back then, home computers and cell phones didn't exist. There were no search engines to give us instant answers. Gerry went to the kitchen and got a piece of bread and a bowl of milk. He dipped small pieces of bread into the milk and dropped them in Tah-Kah's mouth. The crow made gurgling noises. Was he choking? He stretched out his neck, and the bread went down. Then he opened his beak for more. My sisters and I begged to feed him, and Gerry let us try.

Days passed, and Tah-Kah's cries sounded louder and deeper. Gerry kept feeding him bread and milk. Birds aren't mammals! How cow's milk didn't make the poor animal sick, I don't know. In spite of his poor diet, the crow grew incredibly fast. His feathers became long and layered and glossy. One day we noticed bird lice swarming on them. "Take that bird outside!" our mother yelled.

Gerry carried Tah-Kah to the backyard and tossed him into the sky. I screamed when the crow did a somersault and then dove straight down into the bushes. He waddled out, and Gerry launched him into the air again. This time, the bird figured out how to flap his wings. We all took joy in his first flight.

We thought that he'd fly into the woods, never to be seen again. Instead, Tah-Kah took up residence in our yard. He perched on the top bar of the swing set, or a tree branch, or the roof of our house, and looked down on us. When he was hungry, he would land at our feet and squawk. He'd gobble up just about anything we offered him. Mom didn't like us feeding him table food, so my sisters and I dug up worms.

We quickly tired of that. It was much easier to take night-crawlers out of a big tub that belonged to our oldest brother, Bill. He'd gone out at night with a flashlight to find them. Before his fishing trip he discovered most of them missing. "Where'd they all go?" he asked. He was infuriated when he found out we'd fed them to Tah-Kah.

Gerry taught the crow to come to him. "Tah-Kah, caw! Caw!" he'd call, holding out his arm. The bird would land on it, just like in movies. All of us kids imitated him. I loved calling Tah-Kah when I went outside on those summer mornings. He'd swoop down from a tree and land on my outstretched arm. Sometimes his sharp claws scratched my skin, and he often pecked my hand hard while aiming for a treat. But that was a small price to pay to have Tah-Kah as a pet.

Neighborhood children wanted to make friends with the tame crow. They were amazed they could get so close to a wild creature. Tah-Kah wasn't afraid of them and hung around. We had to be extra careful when we played badminton, because he would sit on the net during our games and barely escape getting clobbered. The crow approached domestic animals too, which wasn't always in his favor. He tried to sneak into our dog's kibble bowl, and our mutt almost killed him. That was the first of many close calls.

My father rented the small apartment on the back of our garage to newlyweds Glen and Ruth. Tah-Kah would fly to Glen and land on his shoulder. He'd tug on his moustache and ask for a snack. Glen was kind and fed him blueberries. "I've always wanted a falcon," he confided to me. "Tah-Kah is the closest I'll ever come." But Tah-Kah was unlike a falcon, or any other bird.

He'd hitch a ride on the hood of Glen's car, and when the speed was right, he'd open his wings and take off.

Not everyone got along with him. Glen's wife Ruth was terrified of Tah-Kah. She'd fearfully look around for him as she ran to her car. One time Tah-Kah sat on her open car door and she couldn't close it, so she shook it back and forth. Then he flew to the windshield wipers. When she turned them on, he hung onto a blade as it flipped back and forth. Flip-flop-flip-flop.

Tah-Kah's shenanigans did not amuse my parents. To Mom's dismay, he perched on the clothesline and dirtied the laundry. He also pulled off the pins, and the clothes dropped onto the ground. Dad was disgusted when Tah-Kah began bothering Mr. Rademacher, who lived across the street. The crow would go into his garage, grab small shiny tools off the pegboard, and fly away with them. The day Tah-Kah stole a ratchet end, Mr. Rademacher found it on our lawn and scolded him. The crow must have remembered, for after that he'd fly up behind the man and peck his bald spot!

The weather cooled down and the leaves on the trees turned yellow and crimson. On the first day of school, I was standing at the end of our driveway waiting for the bus, and Tah-Kah landed on my head. "Get off, Tah-Kah!" I shouted. "You're messing up my hair!" I pushed him away.

A couple days later, Gerry asked if I'd seen his crow. I thought back to the day I'd pushed him off my head. "Not since school started."

"I think he's gone forever," Gerry said sadly.

We never saw Tah-Kah again, and I regretted being mean to him.

The ground froze, and the first snowflakes fell. Winter in western New York was brutal that year. Did Tah-Kah survive the blizzards? Maybe he took shelter in a barn. It was probably for the best that he left on his own. There was no way our parents would have allowed him to stay indoors with us.

Years later, I mentioned Tah-Kah to my father. "I wonder why he never came home."

Dad smiled slightly. "That darn crow kept taking Mr. Rademacher's things," he said. "One morning when I got into my car to go to work, Tah-Kah flew in the window and plopped down beside me on the passenger seat. I decided to let him stay there. When I'd driven a good distance from our house, I stopped on the side of the road, and he flew out."

Recently, my sister Barbara came across an old black-and-white photo of Tah-Kah sitting on the badminton net. He looked smaller than I remembered. How had that little crow made such a big difference in our lives? He gave us a special connection to nature that kids today lack. He taught us that birds have definite personalities, just as dogs do.

I kept Tah-Kah's memory alive by writing a children's novel called *Katelyn's Crow*. I based it on some true events, but most of them I made up. In my book, a young girl, someone like me as a child, finds the crow. I hoped to show my granddaughter that there's more to life than her technological gadgets.

twelve

The Blackbird
of Friendship

ANDREA DOERING

My new job was my first fully remote position, where I'd see my colleagues in person only at company-wide meetings several times a year. It was also my first new job in over a decade, and on this, my first visit to the office as an employee, I realized how close to the surface all those "newcomer" feelings were in me. All of a sudden, I had new names to learn, new processes and forms, and who was I going to sit with in the breakroom for lunch? Most of all—would these people even like me? We all knew we could work well together. But what about after work? Traveling to the office meant traveling a thousand miles from home, so I would be here several days, as would other remote-working colleagues. What was the protocol, what was expected for the after-work hours? And would they include me? It was like junior high all over again, and not in a good way.

Well, I didn't have to worry too long, something I am still grateful for. One of my coworkers, Vicki, extended her hospitality before the day's work was done. "Now, Andrea," she said, "where are we going to eat dinner?" And that was that—she graciously enfolded me into the group that often ate together and stayed at the same hotel.

But summertime in the Midwest means long, long evenings full of light, with several more hours after dinner. Vicki already had that covered too. She is an inveterate outdoorswoman, an avid cyclist, kayaker, and geocacher, among other pursuits. She knew of several local nature preserves with walking paths. She invited me to join her at one of them that first evening after dinner. I considered my options, since we had one car between us and I didn't know my way around. I could go back to my clean but generic hotel, with its fluorescent lighting and fake fireplace, and do more work or watch the limited TV options. Or I could step out of my introverted nature and go with Vicki. I chose the walk. And besides, I was curious about where we could go within a city that would feel like a preserve.

That day she chose the ecosystem preserve at a local university. As we entered the shady, tree-filled space, the silence was remarkable. A few minutes earlier we'd been on a busy road, but the trees created an incredible sound buffer, allowing me to pause and appreciate this space even more. Vicki didn't say much, just started off on the path, and for a few minutes I loved the silence. We could hear our own soft footfalls on the loamy path, but that was it. But then that "newcomer" angst started in again, and I found myself nervously chatting and asking her questions, trying to fill up the silence. She answered politely but softly and quickly, and never more than a few words. Suddenly she stopped and pointed out a bird—a beautiful black bird, with red-tipped wings. "Red-winged blackbird," she explained. "Pretty common around here." But wow, what a beautiful bird. We stopped at the edge of a pond and watched as several of them moved in and out of the marshes and trees. It was a joy to watch that flash of red fly by and be able to follow it more easily on its journey. I've since learned we have red-winged blackbirds where I live too—but I only see them in Michigan.

We resumed our walk. Vicki has that quick, quiet sense of the presence of another living thing, and a few minutes later, she pointed toward the pond. She stopped my chattering with a kind "Can you hear that?" Of course I couldn't, I was too busy talking! But I stopped, and yes, I did hear something, a low chirping song coming from the water. "Frogs," Vicki added, nodding her head, like she'd expected them all along. I hadn't heard a frog in decades.

After that I got better about staying quiet and listening and watching, but it was Vicki who did the pointing. We saw turtles, a few rabbits, ducks, and more red-winged blackbirds. We made a few loops around the path, and the second time, in the silence, I was able to appreciate what Vicki had built into her days here at the office. Our work was more cerebral—the work of ideas and data—and decidedly two-dimensional. But after work, she knew it was time for a change. It was time to join the full three dimensions of the natural world and be reminded of beauty, of the rhythms at work that are not made or manipulated by us.

I must not have annoyed her too much though, because walking through nature preserves and along lakeshores became part of our normal routine when we both were at the office for a few days, something we practiced for over a decade together. We trekked through most of the preserves of Grand Rapids, Michigan, of which I'm glad to say there are many! When we traveled to the same conferences around the country, we would generally find a place to take a walk, which almost always included Vicki finding the wildlife. It gave us the time and space to grow a friendship through small conversations followed by comfortable silences, right from the beginning.

It was an unusual start to a friendship, and it was pure grace. Vicki did not have to extend herself to include me in something she clearly loved, something a bit out of the normal "let's have a drink after work" mindset. And she didn't have to continue to invite me into her routines. It let me see more of who she was and what she loved to do in a tangible way.

And I'm going to say the day I spotted a red-winged blackbird before Vicki's hand rose to show me where it was, that was a good day!

thirteen

The Bird Connection

ANDI LEHMAN

Before the Covid pandemic crippled travel and quarantined the world, my husband, Dan, and I vacationed in Europe with our son, an entertainer on the Celebrity cruise line. We woke on the eighth day of our twelve-day journey to find our ship, the *Eclipse*, anchored alongside Port de la Sante in Villefranche-sur-Mer in the French Riveria. We tendered over to shore and boarded a train for the short ride to Monaco.

Hugged by the ever-changing, multicolored Mediterranean, the principality of Monaco oozed turrets and arches and Neo-Romanesque architecture. Tropical plants and green vegetation dotted the rocky cliffs that sloped to the sea, and the treble notes from the birds above and the timpani of the waves crashing below serenaded us like a heavenly choir. No wonder Grace Kelly fell in love with the tiny kingdom and its honorable monarch, Prince Rainier III.

Atop the craggy outcropping called the Roche (the Rock), we admired the stately cream-colored palace before wandering southeast along the high sea wall and through the beautiful park grounds that served as a border for the steep bluffs. A persistent mist dampened ornate iron statues of exotic birds and slicked the cobblestones under our feet. The faint smell of salt permeated the damp air.

A little after 1:00 p.m., sated with fascinating facts about our oceans, we asked a docent at the Oceanographic Museum for the nearest restaurant. He pointed up. On the roof of the museum, an outdoor exhibit called L'île aux Tortues (The Turtle Island) housed several species of turtles and documented their vulnerability. A terraced Italian restaurant adjacent to an interactive turtle-themed playground looked out over the ramparts to the sea.

The rain clouds had scuttled to the east, but a strong wind gave the birds overhead a blustery roller coaster on which to ride. As we walked along the patrol path, we watched the feathered fliers float on the air currents or swoop down over the distant white-capped water to skim the surface for unsuspecting fish. Hustling into the dining area, we chose to stay inside because the balcony furniture was wet, but my seat faced the huge bay of windows that surrounded three sides of the outdoor room.

As we browsed our menus, I was startled by a large seagull who sailed straight into the terrace toward a table closest to the perpendicular wall. Despite the high winds and slippery table-top, he landed deftly on sturdy golden legs and big webbed feet. He stomped about for a few seconds before opening his wide wings and shaking himself off like a damp dog. Suitably wrung out, he hopped down off his perch, marched over to the sliding glass door, and gazed into the restaurant.

"What in the world?" I wondered out loud, and my husband and son turned in their chairs just in time to see the big gull rap his oversized yellow bill three times on the window. He was knocking at the door! He peered through the glass and waited politely for a few seconds before tapping harder and longer.

While I watched him wait, I admired his beautiful markings. In full breeding plumage, his head and throat and undersides were bright white and gave him a snowcapped look on a mountain of beautiful gray wings. His wing feathers, ruffled by the stout wind, rippled in soft gray near his neck and breast and darkened toward his wing tips, where they culminated in black. Folded against his body, the ebony ends were accented on both sides by four perfect white half-moons. Small black pupils in pale yellow eyes stared at the people passing by him on the other side of the door.

When his first two summons produced no response, he strutted back and forth along the length of the big window and then stopped and pecked hard on the clear surface once more. Finally, an aproned man appeared from the kitchen and acknowledged the hungry customer with a smile. He slid open the door, spoke to the gull, and tossed several tidbits onto the table. The bird swiveled, hopped back to his landing zone, and gobbled down the chow.

The waiter stood watching his patron for a moment and then left him to his lunch. I was enchanted. When the big fellow finished, he fluffed up his feathers and ran his beak along the edge of both wings, picking at barbs along the way that must have been out of place.

I noticed a large red dot on his lower bill that I later learned provides a target for baby gulls to peck at when they want their parents to regurgitate food and feed them. The seagull lingered a few moments to see if any more food might be coming, but feeding time was over. With one last glance around the table to see if he had left any crumbs, the graceful bird lifted himself effortlessly up into the mist and over the parapet.

As a wildlife rehabilitator and educator for decades, I knew there had to be a great story behind what we had just witnessed. My son and husband exchanged a look of chagrin that said, "Here she goes again," but I plunged ahead. Braving the language barrier, I asked our waiter about the gull.

"Ahh, yes, yes," he said. "Coco." He motioned toward the entrance. "The sign is there."

In our haste to escape the wind, we had missed a billboard just outside the restaurant. I left the table to go and read it. The heading said "Le goéland" ("the seagull" in French). A magenta bubble in the upper right corner displayed a number, 1.5 meters (or 5 feet), next to a photo of a flying gull with wings extended to their full measure. On the left side, by a close-up photo of the bird, the story of Coco was told briefly in several languages.

It seemed the "strange character" we spied on the terrace had been saved by one of the restaurant's waiters when he injured his feet in some fishing line. Once the seagull recovered, he remembered the kindness of the people on the rooftop of the museum, and for years he continued to return daily to request a meal and stalk along the wall overlooking the terrace and the sea.

Before rejoining my husband and son, I asked to meet the aproned benefactor we had seen earlier. Our waiter disappeared into the back and returned with the fellow, who introduced himself as Hedi. In halting English, he called Coco "lovely," and he added, "He is my friend."

I explained that I, too, rescued injured wildlife and taught people to care about animals. When I asked if I might have permission to tell or write the story of the bird back in the States, Hedi's eyes filled with tears. Nodding his head, he said, "Please," and again, as he shook my hand, he repeated, "Please."

On the train trip back to our ship, I looked through my photos and videos of Coco and Hedi, amazed at the instant connections made by a shared appreciation of an avian species. Perhaps this universal love of birds, I mused, is embedded in us by the Creator of the universe, who knows and loves every sparrow.

But sharing Coco's story at home would have to wait. The idyllic cruise we were enjoying was the last we would take before Covid ground the world to a standstill.

At the height of the first US-mandated Covid quarantine in 2020, I received a call from the regional education director at our public library. Because the branches were closed, she couldn't invite me to come and teach summer programs about animals as I had done for nearly twenty years. But she wondered if I would be willing to write some children's programs, present them live but virtually to families through Zoom, and then post the recordings on the library website for the duration of the season. She asked for seven programs, and she would leave the topic matter to me.

I had never "Zoomed" in my life. And I wasn't wild about being filmed, but I was wild about education, kids, and animals, and I was going wild cooped up in my house with twenty-seven education animals who had nothing to do. So I said yes, and my virtual filming adventure began. In an eighteen-month period, I wrote and hosted fourteen online shows for the libraries featuring my animal partners. One of the shows was called Seaside Surprises and featured several stories about meeting ocean dwellers, including the clever Coco.

As I researched seagulls, I identified Coco as a European herring gull. Multiple species of gulls exist all over the world, and the larger ones, like Coco, can live up to twenty-five or thirty years. I already knew gulls were very clever, but I discovered they can learn behaviors, remember people and things, and even pass on knowledge to others. For example, gulls teach their young to stamp their feet in groups to simulate rainfall and fool earthworms into coming to the surface. They lead their offspring to ploughs in nearby fields and show them how to reap the rewards of unearthed grubs and other tasty invertebrates.

Seagulls mate for life, and, like most birds, they are devoted parents, working together to raise their fledglings. They can drink both salt water and fresh water, thanks to a special pair of salt-removing glands above their eyes. And they are the state bird of Utah, where seagulls once helped farmers eradicate a plague of destructive crickets.

My live and recorded presentations weren't exactly what I had told Hedi I intended to do, but Seaside Surprises included several photos and a short video of Coco, and I shared what I learned about seagulls. I added a coloring page of a seagull to the downloadable packet of activities for children. In a small way, Coco helped mitigate Covid during the summer of 2020 by entertaining and educating our local homebound families.

In 2022, the library system finally resumed in-person programming, and the summer theme was Oceans of Possibility. I decided to revisit some of the material in the Zoom programs from the previous two years. Once more, the story of the rehabilitated seagull was enjoyed by all who heard it. For a second time, Coco's rescue touched children who lived an ocean away from him, highlighting again the amazing connections humans have with and through birds.

When I learned that one of my favorite editors, Callie Smith Grant, was compiling an avian anthology, I decided to submit for her consideration my takeaway from the encounter with Coco. But first, I needed to know what had happened to him and to my fellow bird lovers since our meeting in Monaco. I emailed the restaurant at the address Hedi had given me. And the very next day, a generous person named Guila shared the rest of Coco's story.

Hedi, she related, though obviously devoted to Coco, was only one of several waiters who cared for the seagull we saw at lunch on the museum restaurant terrace. A waiter named Christian had rescued Coco in the late nineties when he found the young bird trapped in the gutter with fishing hooks and nets wound around his body. With the help of a professor at the Center Scientifiques de Monaco, which was located inside the Oceanographic Museum at the time, Christian cut off the nets and removed the hooks from the juvenile gull.

Advised by the professor not to touch the bird unless necessary while he healed (a standard practice in wildlife rehabilitation), Christian released Coco as soon as possible but fed him daily on the terrace. When visitors to the L'île aux Tortues left for the day, Coco would follow Christian around like a puppy as he closed the restaurant. The two forged a trusting friendship—the sweetest gift an animal can exchange with a human.

For years, Coco could be recognized by a red string which was still attached to one of his legs, but after nearly a decade, the colored cord detached, and he looked much like all the other seagulls who lurked around the restaurant patio hoping for food. But only one bird came knocking for his supper every day—the beloved bird I had the privilege to meet.

Christian retired several years ago, and Hedi no longer works at the restaurant, but both men often return to visit their friends. Seagulls still beg for scraps on the rooftop or snatch a morsel of food from unsuspecting customers. And once in a while a new bird ventures to the window and taps with his beak, perhaps recalling the behavior from Coco, who understood that the people here welcomed his kind.

But Coco no longer wings his way onto the terrace to light on tabletops. He was likely in his twenties when I met him—a grandfather of a seagull. When the museum closed during the Covid quarantines, the gulls quit coming. But they remembered, and now they are back.

I, too, hope to go back to Monaco with my husband one day. But if I never return, I will fondly recall the amazing bird and the kind individuals who cared for him. Coco reminded me of something I teach regularly to children: What we love always brings us together.

And a love of birds connects people all over the world.

fourteen

Tweets for Help!

KAREN M. LEET

I feed birds every day. Every single day. I do my very best not to fail them. They count on me for their "daily bread."

I began decades ago when my husband worked as an early morning announcer for a public radio station. One morning I woke to a ferocious spring snowstorm. Snow everywhere. Sigh. I could only hope the eager flower bulbs poking well above ground could survive. Though it did not occur to me to worry how birds would manage to find food.

Turned out my husband's boss at the radio station was also an avid bird person. Not only did he know about birds but he was also a licensed bird rehab expert, specializing in raptors. And what he knew about our central Kentucky region was that the robins were back with us after wintering down South.

So the boss had his announcers on the radio ask listeners to help save the robins by putting out food for them or they wouldn't have any. So that's how and when I began to feed the birds.

My husband's boss said to toss out bits of cut apple and bread pieces, and so I did. Day after day I tossed out their food. And soon they were right there at my back steps waiting for me, expecting me, counting on me for their needs.

But when the snow cleared off, the robins stayed. There they were, waiting on trees and bushes and fences for me and their food. My husband's boss warned us—once the robins have begun to count on us for food, they might starve if we stopped.

And so I kept right on feeding birds.

Word spread about the food supply in my yard, and soon my regulars included numerous other shapes, sizes, and types of birds. Sparrows (three kinds), blue jays, cardinals, blackbirds of several kinds, mourning doves, and of course the robins. A few seasonal drop-ins showed up now and then for snacks—just passing through.

But the regulars settled right in. Mourning doves built a nest in a tree right outside my sons' bedroom window. A pair of wrens settled in on an outside windowsill. A robin couple constructed at one end of our back porch. And at the other end, sparrows designed an impressive condo with space for several families.

With a massive set of branches and bunches of leaves, a strong tree had spread out to help support our porch visitors, who enjoyed the protection.

But our yard wasn't just "for the birds." An impressive assortment of wildlife settled down in and around our yard. A massive oak out front housed up to ten leafy squirrel nests. Chipmunks dug burrows here and there. Teensy mice kept trying to share our basement, and a handful of rabbits browsed our backyard clover.

By night a raccoon waddled down a tree onto our roof and into the front yard, while a huge possum squeezed onto our pie pan bird feeder on its skinny pole.

We were known among critters far and wide for our absolutely every single day feeding station, and so we adapted to all of their needs and lifestyles.

I won't say they were—any of them—tame. None came to eat out of my hand. But most were comfortable with me watching from a reasonable distance. Many came for their food as I tossed it out for them, and I enjoyed watching and listening.

And while I enjoyed the bird identification book my husband's boss gave me, I never became a real birder. I got to know the birds that came most often. But I had to check the book to identify any newcomers.

Though I watched them every day, I never did learn to know them by their calls. But I felt comfortable with their songs. Their music came to me through windows as I worked at my desk or cooked dinner. They were part of my life, part of every day.

Then came the day that startled me out of my routine, out of our comfortable relationship. I was doing my regular chores, living my own life just as they were living theirs . . . when suddenly I heard a bird cry that clutched at my heart.

I knew the moment I heard it. Something was wrong with "my" birds—something was terribly wrong. Before I could wonder what was going on—before I could think or plan, before I had a clue—I was running.

I dashed through the house. I paused only long enough to grab a broom. Don't ask me why I did.

Then I was yanking open the back door to dash out to the porch—just in time I spotted a squirrel scuttling along a branch, heading for the sparrows' multilevel nest, where I knew they'd made their homes and protected their young. Not thinking or planning, I raised my broom, swung it around through the air (unwilling to harm even an invading squirrel), and scared at least a year off that squirrel's life.

"Won't try that again, will you?" I scolded at the retreating squirrel. I lowered my broom-weapon and only then realized that a handful of sparrows sat on nearby branches watching.

They'd gathered there, helpless to stop the squirrel from raiding their nests. In their fear, they'd called. And I'd heard their cries for help.

When I erupted from my house to the porch, door slamming behind me, they'd stayed put on their branches, waiting for me. And as I'd swung my broom to scare off that troublemaker squirrel, not a single sparrow budged. They didn't feel any fear of me or my broom. They'd called me, after all.

And when they called me, their cries touching something in me that recognized their fear and distress, I came.

I stood there looking at them. And they looked back at me as if in silent appreciation and thanks. Then they returned to their lives, and I went back to mine.

But I will never forget that moment of connection, of understanding, of their need and my response. I hope if they ever need me again, I'll instinctively know and respond to their need just as I did that day. There's a connection between us, a connection that is deeper than thought, stronger than logic, and more real than I could ever have known before that moment.

fifteen

Daddy's Red Cap Friends

MELISSA HENDERSON

"Watch out! Here they come! Get ready!" Daddy positioned himself on the top step of the brick porch. He remained motionless
as Mama smiled and alerted him to the hummingbirds headed
for his red baseball cap. If we listened close enough, we could
hear the sound of their fluttering wings approaching.

Each day, after waking from a leisurely afternoon nap, Daddy
and Mama enjoyed sitting outside and watching the variety of
birds that visited the yard. Large trees covered the front of their
home with shade. Neighbors walking by often paused for conversation. Friends and strangers spoke about the beautiful flower
garden that my parents had created. Red petunias, yellow mari-
golds, purple and white snapdragons, and red impatiens covered
the flower bed. Their efforts were rewarded by a "Best Yard in
the Neighborhood" plaque, as designated by the town council.

Mama usually sat in a chair holding a book or newspaper while
Daddy took a spot on the step closer to the flowers. The little

hummers, who usually flew away when someone approached, left the nectar-filled feeder and began to circle Daddy's head. The tiny fliers showed no fear of Daddy or his red cap.

After reading books about hummingbirds, we learned that red is a favorite color of those birds. Daddy taught me to use sugar water with no food coloring when making nectar. He had read somewhere that food coloring might be harmful to the creatures.

He concocted a simple mixture of water and sugar, stirred it together, and poured it into the feeder. With the drink ready for the birds, Daddy would hang their treat in a clear feeder on a shepherd hook pole. Then, we would wait to watch the birds enjoy their find.

Friends and strangers who walked closer to the porch to visit with my parents commented about the hummers. "How do you get them to come close to you? They must like you. What's your secret?"

Daddy would answer, "I sit as still as I can, and the little fellas come to my red cap."

This happened every spring and summer afternoon. The hummingbirds would see Daddy sitting on the step and begin to circle his red cap. They seemed to be saying a quick hello before going back to drink from the colorful flowers or sip nectar from the feeder.

The hummingbirds were not the only ones who enjoyed a delicious drink. On a spring morning, we saw a house finch dipping its beak into the small openings and retrieving nectar. Next, a small green lizard climbed the pole and found its way to the sugar water. Another time, a monarch butterfly paused to partake of the treat while slowly flexing its wings back and forth.

Morning and afternoon, the hummingbirds were regular visitors. When Daddy and Mama were not outside, the little fliers flitted from flower to flower and then to the sugar water. As soon as Daddy put on his red cap and went outside, a flurry of activity began as they rushed to welcome him.

On one particular Tuesday summer afternoon, Daddy was wearing a red sweatshirt and his usual red cap. The hummers circled him from head to toe. The red color caught their attention.

After enjoying the time on the front porch, Mama and Daddy went inside to prepare supper. While sitting at the kitchen table, they heard a surprise sound that caused them to look toward the front storm door.

"What was that? Is someone knocking?" Mama asked.

Daddy went to check. He opened the front door and found a defenseless hummingbird lying on the porch. It had flown into the glass door and became stunned. Daddy called to Mama and they watched as the hummer stayed still. Minutes passed, and they considered how they could help the injured one.

Almost on cue, as Daddy said, "Let's see what we can do for the little guy," the tiny bird jumped to its feet and shook. After recovering, the hummingbird flew to the feeder and drank.

All was well with the hummer.

Daddy and Mama taught me the love of birds. From hummingbirds to cardinals, yellow finches, black-capped chickadees, and more, birds have always brought joy to our family. Our love for birds spurred us to learn about their flying and migration habits, the particular seeds each type of bird likes to eat, and how to show care and kindness to birds and other animals.

We learned there are different varieties of hummingbirds. From the ruby-throated hummingbird with a bright red neck, to the brownish-colored rufous, to the buff-bellied type, each one is unique.

Our family has enjoyed having different pets over the years. Dogs, a cat, a rabbit, and goldfish. Although we didn't consider the hummingbirds as pets, we did treat them as very special because of the joy they brought.

Throughout the years, the small, quick-flying, acrobatic birds brought happiness and thrills each time they arrived. Daddy would put the feeder out in early March. Sometimes people would say, "It's too early. They haven't arrived yet."

Daddy knew. When he put the shepherd hook pole in the flower bed and the blooms started opening, he knew the hummingbirds would be there soon. The special connection Daddy had with all birds, especially those hummers, was a great lesson for everyone. "Take care of the animals. Love them, and they will love you."

If you have a red shirt or a red sweatshirt, wear it, sit on your front porch, and wait. Have patience like my daddy. The arrival of these majestic birds may surprise you.

Daddy and Mama have passed on now. I have that red sweatshirt that he wore. Perhaps one of my sisters has the red cap. Each spring, when I step outside wearing that red sweatshirt, I look for the hummingbirds and remember to sit still and let them find me.

Waiting may be the hardest part, but the reward of seeing those fascinating hummingbirds is worth it.

sixteen

Swallows in Time

BARBARA RAGSDALE

During May and June, I share my postage-stamp-sized front porch with a rickety metal table, two chairs, a brilliant red fire alarm high above the riser door, and a bird nest wrapped nice and cozy around the alarm. The adult birds surprised me when they came flying in to build their temporary home, one bit of mud, grass, and feathers at a time. Once complete, the nest measured about three inches high in the front, floating to the back secured in a tight circle, filling in all the vacant space around the alarm. The clever construction, too high for me to sneak a peek, waited, ready to conceal the precious eggs.

I didn't know much about birds in general, and in particular about the ones swooping in to visit me each day. So, I decided it was time for some expert information from a friend who had been bird-watching for twenty years. "Dan, tell me about birds."

"Well, for one thing, they have wings and fly. Anything else you want to know?"

"Very funny. These birds are building a nest around my fire alarm, and I don't know the species."

"Describe them." Dan was a man of few words. He'd spent years watching eagles' nests and ducks in the flyway patterns and counting birds during certain migrations.

"They move so fast that I can't tell the colors except a golden brown on the breast. Small and busy with a split tail. I think there's a dark stripe under the eyes."

Dan paused a minute. "At this time of year, I would guess they're barn swallows returning from the south—Central America or Mexico. Some consider them a nuisance, since they're prone to return to the same spot for a nest each year, but they will clean an area of flying insects. According to the US Fish and Wildlife Service, once eggs are laid, they are a protected species. Can't destroy a nest just because the birds make a mess on the patio."

"What am I supposed to do? I thought swallows only returned to Capistrano." I could hear him chuckle.

"You and the rest of the world. They're all over North America. If there are eggs in the nest, get out of the way because the parents become aggressive to protect the new birds. Until they hatch and gain adult status, I guess you live with them until instinct tells them it's time to leave and the group welcomes new fliers."

"You've helped me a lot . . . I think." I wanted to protect the birds but wished I could have coaxed them to build somewhere else instead of a fire alarm. As I had learned with wrens, it's almost impossible to redirect that natural nesting desire toward a different protected spot for their eggs. I was really hoping the fire alarm wouldn't go off.

Dan was correct. They were barn swallows. I researched the species to learn more about a bird that can fly and eat at the same time. Their incredible speed makes it difficult to identify colors.

In the shadows I was unable to determine the dark color of the top feathers—black, blue, or brown? Couldn't tell male from female. The front breast color was golden brown, or tawny, as experts described it. Most significant was the dark stripe that masked the eyes, an eerie quality, as though they were staring at me. It reminded me of *The Mask of Zorro*. Eventually, I could see the split tail unique to the swallow.

They had plenty of food, since my property is surrounded by a wilderness area with plentiful mosquitoes and gnats. The birds seemed to be especially busy on the days when lawn workers mowed and weeded, disturbing all the bugs close to the ground.

By the time I realized the nest was under construction, a substantial portion of the mud nursery had been completed. It takes approximately two weeks to fashion the final nest from over one thousand mud pellets, and like adobe homes, the pellets are extremely strong after the mud dries. The activity requires the adult birds to fly constantly, about eighteen hours per day, to deposit one pellet at a time. All of that before any eggs are hatched. I got exhausted just watching them.

Observing the swallows proved a fascinating experience, an up-close look at the instinctive design of one of nature's creatures. The adult birds ignored me while they tended to the business of making a family. I did not know when the eggs were laid, how many were being warmed in the nest, or when they would hatch. Like Dan told me, once the eggs hatched, I was an intruder as far as the birds were concerned. The protective mode, flying directly at my face, was appropriate behavior in their daily feeding routine.

The nest was so carefully crafted that the babies didn't even show their bald heads until they were a couple of weeks old. Even then, it was only for food. Suddenly, parents flapped their wings, gave a twittering call, and a head or two popped up with mouths wide open. It's first come, first served. One bird can't capture enough to feed each one of the hatchlings every time they come to the nest. So the parents, or part of the group, fly in and out all day. A quick transfer of food from parent to baby, and then they leave on another trip for more food.

I happened to be sitting on the porch late one afternoon when the parents flew in and up popped five hungry heads. I kept counting to be sure there were that many because somehow the little ones could shuffle around in the closely compacted environment.

The parents wasted no time feeding and flying. Their wings flapped constantly, and they could pause in the air if the nest was covered by another bird providing a feast of bugs. Descriptions say the birds have weak feet, so perching is momentary, not a lengthy diversion for rest.

Eventually, I was not welcome to sit and watch. Their protective instinct regarded me as an interloper. As the hatchlings grew, the parents became more aggressive about survival. Known for swooping, the adults would fly directly to my face, and I would have to lean out of their way. Though the birds were small, about five inches in height with small beaks, I understood their message. *Stay away.*

Swallows have exceptional frontal and lateral vision. These vision qualities allow them to see and capture prey while flying with their mouths open. Late in the evenings, I could see a group of them circling an area filled with the primary food that was settling to earth for the night. A perfect time for the swallows to feed, because hungry birds waited in the nest.

It was a challenge to determine how old the new birds were. Finally, I saw one sitting on top of the nest, not flying but waiting. Some internal timetable prodded it to leave soon.

Preparation for their long flight required the young ones to perch and practice flapping their wings. I have no idea how fast their wings have to move for them to stay aloft. I did see the swallows using the thermal air currents to circle and rest. Nevertheless, the young birds had to learn how to flap to fly. So flapping came first in the nest and then flying, which some of them were reluctant to try.

While I loved watching the birds grow older, I didn't enjoy the droppings left on the porch. I must admit, this aspect became a nuisance. In fact, I avoided the porch until I knew the birds were in exit mode. It was time for the rest of their journey and another call to my friend.

"Okay, Dan, you told me the birds were protected. What about the droppings?"

"There's nothing protected about the leftovers. It's a nuisance and considered hazardous to breathe. You can put newspaper underneath the nest to catch the droppings and discard it each day."

"Too late for that. There's a considerable pile already. I don't sit out there anymore."

"I assume they're almost ready to leave. After they leave, you should clean the entire area." Dan's words left me tired. No way could I clean the fire alarm. From his description of the process, I figured I'd need a hazmat suit with gown, gloves, and mask.

My trips through the door closest to the nest were rare as I chose instead to exit the apartment through the garage to my car. Nevertheless, curiosity piqued my interest to check on the birds. Sneaking a peek one evening long after the sun had gone down, I was startled to see all five new adults perched on top of the nest, staring at me. In the dim yellow light, they looked like five angry gargoyles hunched together, the prominent black stripe a menacing feature. They never moved, just looked. I stared back. *Yep, I'm still here, but you're going to be leaving soon,* I thought.

The next morning, I left early without any thought of the birds. Back home later in the day, I discovered three of the birds had left the nest, joining their parents in a round-robin circle, swooping and flying, urging the remaining two timid ones out of the nest. It took a lot of circles. Reminded me of parents calling to a child to jump in the pool. "Come on. I'll catch you." The remaining birds seemed to be just as skeptical as that child standing on the side of the pool.

The parents flew directly to the nest, paused with a furious flapping of the wings, and then zipped away. Their urgent message said, "This is how it's done. It's time for us to go, and you need to come with us." I had to step out of the way several times as they bombarded me with diving attempts straight to my face.

By late afternoon, all the birds had left the nest. I could see them circling around, snagging the abundant food. As the weather chilled, I realized the swallows had followed their instincts. It was warmer elsewhere.

For now, my patio area is clean, but I expect to see them building again. As always, it will be a quiet, concealed ritual until nearly complete. Then, I will watch quietly, as a friend not a predator, and wish them well for another year.

seventeen

The Owl Prayer

DELORES E. TOPLIFF

My eleven-year-old son's feet thundered across our porch. He flung open our door, kicked off his boots, and tossed his hat onto the couch before his face rounded the doorframe. Andrew was home from school.

"Mom, I prayed for an owl to keep as a pet," he said, all smiles. "I told the kids in class, and we know God will send one. We can't wait!"

His dark eyes danced, but mine didn't. No parent wants to see their child disappointed. I teach in our Christian school and believe in answered prayer, but I wished my son had prayed for something that seemed easier to me, like a new fishing pole or bicycle or trip to the beach—instead of asking him to send an owl to a valley that had none. That year, I had taught a junior hunter safety course for the Fish and Wildlife Service, so our students could hunt and fish. We had plenty of moose, bear, deer, foxes, and migrating swans, geese, and other birds—but no owls.

Days passed. Maybe Andrew would forget the owl. But no. "Sometimes it takes God a while to answer prayers," he reminded me.

Then one snowy cold evening as I prepared to grade schoolwork at home, I found I'd left my grade book on my desk at the school up the hill. Maybe my oldest son would get it for me.

"Andrew, would you please run up to my classroom and bring back my grade book?"

"Are you sure you need it?" He had settled in for the evening too. He clearly wanted to grumble but didn't. Shoulders slumped, he slipped into his coat and boots and headed out the door. As he trudged up the hill, he saw an unusual shape on top of the round bush near our path. When he tossed a twig that direction, the shape rose, flapped its wings, and parted Andrew's hair before crashing into our porch and falling down, stunned. Andrew cupped it in his hands and ran inside shouting, eyes wide like someone who has just seen God.

"Mom, Mom, God sent me my owl!" Our family surrounded him, our eyes filled with happy tears and our hearts overflowing with thankfulness.

The owl was a little larger than Andrew's hand. Its feathers were chocolate brown with dark markings around its glowing gold eyes. Before long, it perched on Andrew's finger and let him smooth its wings.

We phoned our friends at Fish and Wildlife and sent them pictures. They said it was a northern pygmy owl and gave us permission to keep it. "It's probably sick or wounded," the head officer said. "It's unusual for them to come close to habitation."

We didn't see anything wrong with the bird but were happy with their decision.

We placed the owl in a large rabbit cage lined with straw and small evergreen branches. We asked the Fish and Wildlife officers what kind of food and care the owl needed. They suggested sardine pieces from a can and water and milk from an eyedropper. Andrew's younger brother, Aaron, caught a mouse a day to feed the owl. He snapped it up to eat it fast.

School classmates came to our home, admiring this answer to prayer. Although there were no owls in our valley, they had been sure one would come.

As they enjoyed milk and cookies, they worked on finding the right name. "Flash," "Arrow," "Wind," they suggested.

"Whoosh," Andrew's friend Ben said. "That's the sound it makes when he spreads his wings and flies fast."

"Yes, Whoosh," we all agreed.

Whoosh could turn his head almost completely around when he looked at us. It hurt our necks when we tried to do that.

After school each day, friends came by to watch Whoosh preen his feathers and sharpen his razor talons. He stayed content standing free on top of his rabbit cage most of the time. Andrew covered the cage with a towel when it was time for Whoosh to sleep.

We all enjoyed Whoosh, but Andrew was the only one who handled him. The owl could rip most things apart but didn't hurt my son with his sharp beak or slashing talons.

Andrew took Whoosh to school for the elementary students to see. "He's so soft and fluffy," their teacher said, reaching forward to touch him.

"Please don't do that," Andrew said. "He obeys me, but he's still wild."

"But he looks so gentle," the woman said, reaching forward.

Faster than our eyes could follow, Whoosh snapped and nipped her finger hard before resting on Andrew's hand again.

"Ouch. I should have listened," the woman said, holding her finger.

All that next week, Whoosh stayed in our home, but at times his head seemed to droop.

"Mom, do you think Whoosh is okay? Do you think he's sad?" Andrew asked.

I waited awhile to answer. "Son, you love him and give him great care, but he probably misses his family and friends. He might be lonely for woods and skies and moonlit treetops."

Andrew talked to our Fish and Wildlife friends again.

"Whoosh might have been sick when you found him," one said. "Maybe that's why he came close to humans. Maybe now he can live free in the forest again."

Andrew loved having Whoosh but wanted him to be happy too. He thought it over for several days and then invited his school friends to see Whoosh one last time to say goodbye. We took pictures.

"Goodbye, Whoosh. We'll miss you," Aaron said.

Toward sunset that night, Andrew asked our family to walk with him to the end of our fields where the woods began. He held Whoosh in his hands and asked God to take good care of him. Then he lifted him up to the sky and let him go.

At first, Whoosh flew in circles above us. Then he headed west toward purple hills. I put my arm around my son and wiped my eyes. I could see Andrew growing more into a man.

We're thankful God listens to prayers. I think he often puts requests in our hearts that he wants to answer.

We were happy Whoosh came to live with us but also that he could be free again to fly above the treetops in sunshine or through starlight.

Even better, that next summer, two pairs of owls came to live in our valley. We got close enough to watch but didn't try to catch them. And we've had owls here every summer since.

eighteen

Dove in the Window

BETTY L. CARTER

I was sitting with my husband, Jim, at the hospital once again. He had been in and out of the hospital for the last three years with so many health issues, one thing right after another. I held his hand and asked if I could get him anything before I left to go home.

He said, "I'd sure love to have something sweet!" I was not surprised because he loved sweets better than anything.

"I'll go down to the vending machine and get you something. Anything in particular?" I asked.

"Anything sweet will do!" He looked past me to the window-sill and said, "Why, look. There's Priss. You can go with her, Priss! You're a free spirit!"

Miss Priss was our twenty-three-year-old tabby cat who had passed away in Jim's arms back in February. Today was May 21. Jim had loved her and she loved him. She was an extraordinary pet who sensed when you were sick and would come and sit with you until you felt better.

I looked out the window, but of course there was nothing there. I started out the door, and he said, "She's following you out!"

I went on down to the lobby and got Jim a couple bags of M&M's. He ate most of one pack while I put off leaving. I didn't want to go but at the same time wanted to drive the hour home before dark.

We hugged and kissed goodbye, and the last thing Jim said to me was, "I'll love you forever and always!"

"I love you too!" I said. And slipped out the door.

I pondered over him seeing Miss Priss as I headed down the road. He'd said she hadn't come back in the room with me when I returned from the lobby, and I wondered what it could mean. I couldn't bear the thought of going home to an empty house, so I stopped by our son's to spend the night. I got the phone call at 3:30 the next morning. He was laughing and talking with his nurses one minute, and the next minute my Jim was gone.

We had been married for sixty-three years. He was only seventeen and I a mere fifteen on April 16, 1960, when we said our vows. But we both knew without a shadow of a doubt that we had found our forever love. We had four children, three boys and a girl, all of them gone from home and most with children of their own. As most everyone does, we had our ups and downs, but we loved each other fiercely till the last day. Jim was one of the good guys. A beloved husband, father, and granddad, and he loved the Lord with all his heart.

Time passed as I struggled to live without him. It was not getting much easier.

Later that year, in the midst of mourning the loss of Jim, our middle son had to have emergency surgery and almost died due to diverticulitis and a ruptured colon. I sat at the hospital with him and his wife Debbie every day as he slowly recovered.

I had signed up for a barn quilt painting class some time back at our local extension office just to keep my hands busy. I love to draw and paint and thought maybe the class would help with my grief. There was a constant ache in my heart, and it was hard to face each day without Jim.

As time approached for the class, I decided not to go. I thought with the stress of losing Jim and almost losing our son, it would be too much.

Our daughter Mindy said, "Mom, it would be good for you to go . . . you need this class! It will help you. Please tell me you'll go."

So I went! The room was full of people picking out their designs. I chose a pretty design with light blue and dark blue colors. It was called "Dove in the Window." We were allowed two evenings to work on our project. The second night as I finished, I thought it needed a little something extra, so I added four good-sized dots in the white spaces.

The instructor said, "Of all the people that have painted this particular design, no one has added the pretty dots, so you get to rename it. What will you call it?"

"Hmmm," I said. "Four dots, four children! I think I'll call it 'Jim's Tribute.'"

The next evening, after sitting all day with my son and daughter-in-law at the hospital, I got in my Kia to head home. I was thankful to God that Jeff was doing so much better.

It was a scorching hot August day. As I slowly backed out of my parking space and put the Kia in drive, I looked out the windshield, and there sat a dove on my hood. I grabbed my camera and started snapping photos. The dove was in no hurry and sat there while I took four pictures. In the final picture, it turned and looked me in the eye and held my gaze for a long minute before it gracefully flew away.

I could scarcely breathe. Covered in goosebumps or glory bumps, I sat there for another minute or two gathering myself together before heading home.

And I thought, *My God is all powerful and can do all things! I know this was you, Lord! Thank you, thank you! Glory to God!*

And I've been rejoicing ever since!

nineteen

Of Birds and Men

PATRICIA AVERY PURSLEY

My love of birds started when I was about eight years old. After every Christmas in Michigan, Dad would haul the Christmas tree, wayward tinsel still dangling, into the backyard and prop it up in a snowbank against the fence. My mother gave my sister and me bowls of popcorn and cranberries to string at the kitchen table. We bundled up and hung the garlands on the tree. Back inside, we stood impatiently by the kitchen window, scanning the sky. We were thrilled when birds began to gather on the fence and fly to the treats. Against the white snow, the deep red cardinals with big black eyes were the real showstoppers. It might have been a scene from a Monet winter painting.

My bird-watching continued, and decades later in Fort Worth one cold December, a fluorescent green parakeet showed up at my bird feeder. The sparrows didn't seem to mind and occasionally leaned in as if to comment, "Who's the guy in green?" Then there was the rare sight in our Colorado yard of five—count them, five—intensely blue mountain bluebirds bathing in our birdbath. Splish-splash, and it wasn't even a Saturday night!

Meanwhile, in Colorado Springs, my friend Linda had a moving experience with a local woodpecker shortly after her dad passed away. The woodpecker came to sleep under the eave outside her bedroom window. He was there for months, bringing her a measure of comfort. Every night she shined a flashlight on his resting place to see if he was there. When her grandson came to visit, they checked with the flashlight, and sure enough, the woodpecker was tucked in for the night. Her grandson was enthralled! Linda said she was tearful when the woodpecker moved on, but she held the memory in her heart. A keepsake memory for her and her grandson. It seemed that an ancient liturgy had come to life: "The breath of all life praises Your Name!"

Years later, a brilliant green hummingbird flew through our open patio door and was convinced he could escape through the skylight. Wobbling atop an eight-foot ladder, I finally came close enough to reach out and rescue him. How do you describe clasping a handful of feathers? Wonder upon wonders.

Bird-watching continued across the sea when my husband, Tom, and I were entertained by gray Parisian pigeons splashing in the reflecting pool outside the Louvre, as though paying homage to the arts. Down the avenue, the grays had their own version of cafe culture, nibbling croissant crumbs and sipping water near an open fire hydrant. And closer to home at the Bronx Zoo, the resident peacocks paraded next to us on the walking paths as if they owned the place. With heads held high, they strutted within pecking distance of our picnic table, looking for donations.

Back home again in Texas, we witnessed the changing of the guard as tiny migrating yellow finches flitted through the hedge and took turns at the feeder. However, none were as bold as the cardinals or as audacious as our gang of thieving crows.

Every year, our resident cardinals' nest is tucked into a thick jasmine vine high atop our trellis. I've read that cardinals are monogamous and keep the same mate for life. We saw the male flying back and forth to the nest, probably carrying seeds to feed his mate. One afternoon I was having a sandwich at the dining room table, and nearby my cat, Isabella, was sunning on her perch in the window. I spotted our flashy red male and his mate stationing themselves in a pine tree. Always in territorial mode, he spotted Isabella through the window. Turning his head this way and that, showing off his black mask, he seemed to be carefully planning his strategy. Plan A: He was going to rid this cat from his property. Red calculated his odds of survival and angle of attack, then he and his mate swooped into the holly bush outside the window. He proceeded to repeatedly launch himself in a blaze of red feathers against the glass, then dart back to the holly. Isabella shivered with excitement at her luck. Dinner! And right outside the window! Like any good wife driving from the passenger seat, Red's mate perched nearby chirping instructions: "Be careful! Not too close!" Isabella and I stayed frozen in place as this offensive played out.

Isabella hoped upon hope that Red would somehow come within striking distance on her side of the glass. Her belt already had notches for numerous geckos, and she was looking to add this prize cardinal. Meanwhile, apparently on the off chance that the cat could be nearsighted, this bold cardinal proceeded to Plan B: He hopped right down on the window ledge. He gave Isabella an up-close, beak-to-nose examination. His beak on one side of the glass placed directly onto her nose on the other as if to challenge her. None of us moved a muscle for several seconds. Red's bird brain finally concluded that the cat was probably chicken. The family nest was saved for the day. While this old cat shivered with excitement, eyeing the possibility of red cardinal for dinner, she too had calculated her odds and was sure she would get him next time.

On the other hand, the incredibly large, glossy black crows are a different breed of imperialists, and they too mate for life. Officially, a flock of crows is known as a murder. I say call it like it is: a gang of bandits. Our close-knit gang has a hideout somewhere in the thick forest around our neighborhood. They come for the peanuts we scatter for the cat-stalking cardinals and the rare peanut-fed blue jays.

After chasing the crows out of our yard in vain for weeks, my husband, the new sheriff in town, was tossing out peanuts when he spotted their lookout. Just like in the Old West movies, the lookout was suited up in black atop a neighboring house on the next block. Astonished at their level of organization, Tom dubbed them the Crow Brothers. The lookout squawked, "Peanuts, peanuts, Pursley one block over!" They have a dossier on us. Like the stagecoach robbers in Old West movies galloping out of the hills, the Crow Brothers whooped and hollered, "Hand over your peanuts. All of them!" As the loud and obnoxious gang descended on our yard, they posted two lookouts to cover the charge. One brother perched in our Chinese fringetree; another stood guard high on a pine branch. Once on the ground, they looked oddly oversized. While three or four brothers snatched multiple peanuts each and made a run for it, the lookouts hung back to cover the rear, squawking ominous warnings over their shoulders as they all flew off. We tried tossing the peanuts under the hedge to hide them, but the wily Brothers could easily spot the treats and go in for the steal. We have since surrendered and now toss a few extra peanuts out for the gang. I understand now why a flock of crows is called a "murder"!

So whether the magnificent feathered creatures bring us beauty, comfort, or fun, as Peter Harris wrote in his book *Under*

106

the Bright Wings, "Much of the beauty of the Woodlark's song, or the colors of a Bee-eater's plumage, goes well beyond what might be seen as necessary . . . and speaks of the artistic activity of a creator working to a different set of priorities than what is merely useful or efficient."[2]

twenty

The Renegade Parrots

LONNIE HULL DuPONT

In San Francisco, a flock of wild, green parrots lives near the bay. Nobody knows for certain how they got there—after all, parrots are not native to Northern California. One rumor is that a pet shop burned down and these parrots managed to save themselves and become a renegade flock. Whatever the reason, this flock has been living on Russian Hill and Telegraph Hill for many years, flying between the two hills, chattering for those lucky enough to see or hear them.

I lived on Telegraph Hill for many years in the North Beach neighborhood of the city. During my first six years, I heard about the parrots, but I never saw them. I'd heard of people seeing them, but I never talked to anyone who had. In fact, I had one friend who was convinced that the existence of the wild parrots in San Francisco was an urban myth.

In my fifth year in San Francisco, I married. My husband and I stayed in my original apartment on the side of Telegraph Hill for the next few years. This was a golden time. We were true, dewy-eyed San Franciscans, in love with our quirky neighborhood, with the billowing fog that burned off by noon, and with each other. We were in good health and crazy about life. We felt unbelievably blessed.

Each morning for exercise, I took walks up Telegraph Hill, one of the city's several steep hills where sometimes the sidewalks are flights of stairs. At the top of Telegraph Hill, I'd watch the sun rise out of the Bay, illuminating the dozens of Chinese neighbors scattered around the hilltop doing group calisthenics or tai chi. I'd circle Coit Tower, then head back down the hill through a grove of bottle brush trees and bushes of holly. At a short group of stairs, I would always stop, look around at the beauty, and sigh with pure San Francisco pleasure. Then I'd descend the stairs and wind my way home.

One morning, I'd walked my walk, climbed the hill, nodded to some of the Chinese exercisers, and headed down through the grove to the stairs. As usual, I stopped at the top of the steps, looked out over the Bay, and took a deep breath.

This morning, however, I prayed inside, saying how grateful I was for my life. I had had difficult years as a young adult, years full of stress and loneliness, punctuated with the untimely deaths of several people I loved. I felt God had been with me through all of that, and now I felt happier and healthier than I ever had. I felt as if for now I was coasting. I stood for a long time, letting the blessings of my life scroll through my mind. Then I looked up at the sky and said out loud, "Thank you, God."

When I started to take a step down the stairs, I suddenly heard such a racket overhead that I stopped short and looked up. There, surging up over the crest of the hill behind me, were the parrots. I was stunned.

I watched the neon streaks of green against a dazzling blue sky and heard the screaming, squawking chatter of fifteen to twenty parrots in formation racing over me, heading west toward Russian Hill. I looked around quickly to see if anyone was around—I so wanted to share this moment! But there was nobody else. Later my friend who didn't believe the parrots existed would quiz me in great detail as to what I saw. And she never did believe me.

But I saw them. I heard them. It took only seconds, and they flew directly over me immediately after I had thanked God out loud.

And as that renegade flock of parrots became smaller in the sky, quieter, I heard the Voice inside that I've learned to trust over the years say loud and clear: You're welcome.

twenty-one

Something to Crow About

DAVID KITZ

If you asked me if I like birds, without hesitation I would answer, "Yes." If you asked me if I like crows, the quick answer would be, "Not so much."

I suppose it's their voice that irritates me the most. They can't seem to hit the right note. Their early morning cawing drives me insane. There's nothing quite as irritating as a crow's relentless caw near your window as you try to get that well-earned hour of extra sleep on a Saturday morning.

I'm convinced someone should invent a beak muzzle for crows. For humane treatment, the muzzle should be designed to allow crows to peck their food and eat normally, but it would be instantly activated the moment they try to caw.

Surely with all the recent improvements in technology, such a device is possible. With the right marketing team, I'm sure millions of these devices would be sold. Think about the sales that a beak muzzle commercial during the Super Bowl could generate!

And consider the prestige. The inventor of a beak muzzle for crows would undoubtedly be awarded the Nobel Peace Prize—auditory peace. Saturday morning peace. Can there be a higher honor?

But a few years back I had a dramatic change of heart about crows.

It all started on a lazy Saturday afternoon in the summer. I was sitting in my living room, watching a different flock of birds—the Toronto Blue Jays. As I recall, those birds were in a tense match with their rivals the Yankees.

Suddenly, *KA-BANG!*

The whole house shook. My wife came running into the living room. "What happened?"

After a moment of stunned silence, I replied, "I have no idea."

"Well, something hit the house," she insisted.

"I think it hit the front window," I offered.

Together we rushed over to our living room picture window. The window itself looked fine. But there on our front lawn lay a crumpled heap of black feathers.

I slipped on my shoes and headed out for a closer look. Sure enough, it was a big crow. The afflicted bird didn't struggle to escape as I approached. He was in no condition to do so. His left wing rested in a splayed-wide state on the grass, while the other wing was tilted up awkwardly but held close to the body. His head and neck were skewed grotesquely to one side.

I crouched down for a better look. That's when our eyes met.

Until that moment, I had been thinking, *Oh good, I'll be rid of one of these pesky nuisances. And if he isn't dead, out of mercy I'll finish him off and bury him in the backyard.*

But his eyes said something quite different. He was still alive, and he clearly fixed his right eye on me. At the same time, his beak hung open as he frantically gasped for air. With each gulp he seemed to be saying, "Mercy! Mercy! I didn't mean to collide with your window. Mercy!"

We communed eye to eye like that for a few seconds. Then I repented of my murderous thoughts. I said a silent prayer for good health for my hapless feathered friend, stood up, and walked back into the house.

I discussed the state of my fallen comrade with my wife, Karen. After considering all the options, we both agreed it was best to leave the crow exactly where he was. Perhaps he was just winded and would recover—a rather unlikely prospect, I thought. But there was no harm in waiting.

I resumed watching those other birds—the Blue Jays. After a particularly tense inning of play, I got up to check on the casualty in the front yard. He was gone. I walked out to the spot where he once lay to confirm his disappearance. I looked around the area. No sign of him.

As I reentered our home, I had a smile on my face. I felt strangely happy that the bird had made good his escape without any intervention on my part.

I considered this event to be unusual but not particularly impactful—except for the crow. And it certainly didn't change my opinion about crows. But the story doesn't end there.

About ten days later, early in the morning, I found myself standing on my front lawn at about the same place where my fallen friend had landed. I was deep in thought—not about crows and their place in the world but rather that great esoteric question common to man: *Can I put off cutting the lawn for another day, or should I tackle this chore today?*

Suddenly a crow interrupted my contemplation. He fluttered down from a large maple in my neighbor's yard and landed on the front porch. From there he scooted closer onto the driveway. Then from there this audacious crow walked over to me on my front lawn.

I had never been approached by a crow before. I felt quite uncertain how I should respond. To be blunt, I was thunderstruck.

He, on the other hand, seemed completely at ease. He stopped about a meter from me. Then he looked me over as only a crow can do, cocking his head first to one side, then the other. For a second time our eyes met. That was when he began to speak, not with his squawky annoying voice but with his eyes. Here's what I heard him say—mind to mind:

Sorry for dive-bombing your house the other day. That was dumb of me.

Your mercy is appreciated. Thanks for praying for me.

As you can see, I'm fine now.

And with that said, he turned abruptly, flapped his wings a few times, and ascended to his lofty perch in my neighbor's maple tree.

As for me, I returned to my house, a humble man.

Since that day I've thought a good deal about my interaction with that crow. Skeptics might well doubt the truth of my account. Can I prove that the crow that walked up to me was the same crow that collided with my window? No, I can't. I can't distinguish one crow from another. I can't even tell if the crow I encountered was male or female. But I do know that researchers have found that crows have keen skills of human recognition and recall. Furthermore, I've read and heard countless stories that highlight the intelligence of these birds.

Accuse me of putting words in a bird's beak if you like, but I believe that bird descended to my level and walked over to me with the express purpose of communicating with me in the best way he (or she) could. And he succeeded in his mission.

The Gospel of Luke records the account of Jesus healing ten lepers (Luke 17:11–19), and that only one returned to give thanks. I showed mercy to just one crow, and he returned to express thanks. Which is the superior species?

About 5:30 this morning I awoke to the cawing of a crow. And you know something? For me, that bird hit all the right notes.

I appreciate getting love notes—thank-you notes—even from a crow.

twenty-two

Listen to the Seagulls

MELODY CARLSON

My mother-in-law, Patsy, was a difficult woman. And pretty much everyone who knew her knew it. I learned early on to watch my step around this somewhat erratic woman, but I didn't fully understand what was going on until much later in life. With time and trust, Patsy divulged how she'd grown up in a terribly dysfunctional home. And I began to understand that, possibly due to her troubled childhood and DNA, she was extremely bipolar and consequently very unpredictable. You never knew what to expect with her.

Well, unless you were conversing with her about nature. Patsy adored nature. She revered all of God's creation . . . vegetable, mineral, animal. I quickly learned to respect her expertise, and that as a well-read, intelligent woman, she didn't like to be questioned. She was the authority, and she often proved it. But her deep connection to nature was one of the things I loved best about her. It was her happy place.

Patsy's favorite part of nature was birds. She loved birds of all kinds! And she seemed to know everything about her fine feathered friends. After only a few years of being her daughter-in-law, I made a valuable discovery. I could utilize her love of birds as my escape hatch. You see, Patsy would often call me when she was in a disturbed state of mind. Whether she was sharing information I didn't care to hear or making an accusation I didn't believe was accurate, it could get awkward.

So one day, while listening to her grousing about something, I noticed some cute little birds splashing in a puddle of water outside my kitchen window. At this stage of life, I was more caught up in raising my children than paying close attention to birds. But I described the birds to her, feigning more interest than I actually felt. "They've got these neat white vests and little black hoods." Suddenly the tone of her voice changed. "Oh, those are Oregon juncos," she said pleasantly. I'd never heard the word *junco* before and thought she was kidding. "Junk oh?" I asked. "Why would you call this cute bird junk?" She just laughed and explained, even spelled the name. We chatted a bit more about birds, and that was that. The unpleasant conversation was forgotten.

I had a new tool, a way to segue from a disturbing topic. By simply describing a bird I'd seen or asking a bird question, I could often distract her. She would identify the bird and go into detail about it. And sometimes she'd call me and simply chat about whatever birds she was feeding in her backyard. I learned from her to keep binoculars and a bird book handy. And I became a bit of a bird nerd too.

Years passed, and Patsy and her husband Frank retired and relocated to the Oregon Coast. The birds there were slightly different from the inland birds she'd known so well, but she quickly learned all about the beachy birds and, armed with binoculars and feeders, befriended them. And Frank took up carving them in wood.

But Patsy's favorite bird on the Oregon Coast was the humble seagull. She helped me to see the seagull with new eyes too. She pointed out how each one was unique, with different coloring variations. She described how they had different personalities too. She even had names for some of them. She found them to be amusing and entertaining.

Toward the end of her life, although she and Frank were becoming less mobile, Patsy loved being taken to the Siuslaw River in Florence, Oregon, where they would park near the water's edge. Using her walker, Patsy would slowly meander to the end of the long floating dock and happily feed the squawking seagulls.

In her last days, she required a wheelchair, but Patsy insisted on going down there. She needed to visit and to feed her birds. It was the highlight of her day . . . of her life even. Her happy place. But the years caught up, and her health declined, and Patsy passed away . . . and Frank shortly thereafter.

When it came time to scatter their mother's ashes, her children all agreed that the end of her seagull dock was the place. Patsy's three sons were assigned the task. I went with them but remained back on the dock, watching from a distance as the three men carried the ashes to the end. As they walked, I noticed a flock of seagulls gathering in the sky. Probably two dozen or more. I assumed the birds expected to get some food. Seagulls can be ravenous birds. But these gulls remained in the sky, just circling overhead.

I kept an eye on the gulls as Patsy's middle-aged sons scattered their mother's ashes. I felt concerned that the seagulls would think the men were throwing out food and swoop down upon them like a scene from *The Birds*. But the seagulls stayed in the sky, almost reverently, slowly circling. As they flew, they let out this mournful sort of wailing sound. A haunting cry that was nothing like the noisy squawking I'd heard from seagulls before. It was an eerie sound, as if the birds were mourning . . . as if they somehow knew that their good friend Patsy was gone.

We all talked about this strange phenomenon afterward. We agreed that we'd never heard that kind of seagull sound before. And then we began remembering the good things about a woman who had left a mixed bag of memories behind. Thanks to those seagulls, it became a healing time, a time to remember their mother, the troubled woman who had always loved nature and birds . . . and was now free from her burdens, flying above with wings of her own.

twenty-three

Safe at Home

ROSE McCORMICK BRANDON

Life requires us to fill many roles. One day we may find ourselves in grubby clothes operating a lawn mower, and the next in a gown headed to a gala. Sometimes it's the simple, unexpected roles we play that add the most charm and leave the deepest impression.

One warm afternoon, I fell into the role of bodyguard to a baby robin. A family of robins had nested in the birdhouse we had nailed to a post that stood in front of the lilac tree. The post was about five feet high, tall enough to discourage our cat and the neighbor's cat from climbing up and disturbing the bird family that we hoped would find the house and move in. Since observing several open beaks protruding through the porthole, we had kept a close eye on the little family's comings and goings.

After uprooting a few plants from one area of the yard and moving them to another, I sat under a tree with a cold drink. I soon heard chirping, not the usual happy chirps one hears from robins on a rainy day, but anxious chirping, like a mother calling to a child in danger. "Stay away from the busy street!"

The sounds were coming from two adult robins sitting on the back fence. The object of their concern? One of their babies was stranded on our picnic table. Although I couldn't read the expression on Baby's face, his body language said he was terrified. Alone. Away from home and needing the intervention of his parents. Trying out his independence had been fun, but how to get back to the nest—that was the problem. He flapped his tiny wings but didn't seem to have the courage to lift off. His voice hadn't yet developed, but his faint cries reached the ears of his parents and mine too. They, at one point, flew over to Baby and appeared to urge him to eat the worms they carried in their beaks, sustenance for the journey back home perhaps. He didn't take the bait.

The adults, maintaining their vigil on the fence, changed their terrified chirps to encouraging cheeps. "You can do it," they seemed to say. "You were meant to fly." Frightened by the outcome of what had seemed such an exciting adventure, Baby hesitated. After a long pause, he flapped just enough to lift off from the picnic table and land on the grass. Not the safest place. Seeming to sense the danger of a lurking cat, he took flight again and aimed for the rhubarb patch, closer to home. He landed on the crest of a large leaf, where he again seemed to freeze with fear. By this time, my husband had joined me on guard duty. He coaxed Baby off the leaf and onto his hand. Gently, so as not to frighten him, he moved the baby robin to the fence near the birdhouse, his family home. Still, he was petrified and unable to make the short trip home. The parents continued their on-again, off-again lectures. They flew around to demonstrate how this flying business would come naturally to him if he would just try.

Then Jack, our orange tabby, showed up. And this was when guard duty took on a serious note. Our Jack likes birds a lot more than he should. He often sits on the front porch glaring at their activities in the maple tree. He has managed to grab and maul a couple of them before we could intervene. Whenever I saw him focusing on the maple tree, I would clap my hands and yell to distract him. I bought a bell and attached it to his collar so the birds could hear him approaching and fly away. That bell lasted one day. Jack spent hours on the front porch pulling and twisting the collar with his paws until he managed to get it off. Aside from his bird-hunting ways, Jack is a good and dependable cat who snuggles with us when we are sick and sits in a comforting way with his much-older pal next door. But he is not kind to birds.

Noticing that the baby robin was vulnerable, Jack crouched in attack position nearby. He meant to destroy Baby. *If Jack has his way,* I thought, *we'll find this robin deposited at our back door, a gift from a predator who believes he's done a fine day's work.* Jack often puts mice and moles and the occasional unfortunate bird on the step at the back door where we will be sure to find them. He is proud of his hunting ability.

I clapped loudly and shooed Jack away while my husband watched over the scene by the fence. The parents had quieted. Maybe the quiet gave Baby time to think and really consider his options. Should he use his wings and fly with confidence or accept that his life was soon to come to a dismal end?

We waited. Jack left. He lost interest in Baby and turned his attention elsewhere. The tiny robin gained enough courage to fly the short distance from the fence to the top of the nest. He sat there for a few seconds, relieved. Then, quick as a wink, he turned upside down and tucked himself through the round opening to the nest. The adults flew swiftly after him, into their sanctuary. They had come close to losing one of their babies. They needed time to breathe, time to get over the trauma of what might have been.

I know that feeling. Our youngest, eager to show off his new driving skills, recently overturned our truck and miraculously escaped without a scratch. Like me, the robin parents must have laid down the law—no more flying/driving—until tomorrow. Or at least until I catch my breath!

twenty-four

Feathers from
a Winter Moon

GERALD FLEMMING

In the last fifteen years, my wife and I have made trip after trip to Goodwill and the Salvation Army. We've mostly made good on our promise to empty our basement of anything we thought other people could use. Everything from old clothes to antique furniture we thought we might restore but didn't. Hopefully our things found homes with people who had more time and patience.

Amongst those basement shadows, back by the antique Christmas ornaments and the rack of seasonal coats, is a slightly warped and rickety old wooden folding table. Every now and then I'll go down, gently unfold the table, and drag my fingers across the indented scrape marks that were put there by his talons. It still gives me a shiver.

Late one winter evening, a younger me was working at my old walnut veneer desk. The sprawl across the huge top was as listed: black coffee in a big mug, multiple Bible translations, a laptop, colored pens, and a journal. I've been blessed to spend my adult life as a Christian songwriter and was, at this moment, struggling between the cadence and the theology of a line.

Suddenly, I was jolted out of my waning focus by what sounded like a person falling and thudding on the floor. I bolted up and scrambled through the folding doors into the dining room. I heard Allison call out my name in shocked concern. As I rounded the corner into the living room, she was also scrambling toward me as we barely avoided running into each other.

"Are you all right?" I asked.

She shook her head. "Me? I thought that was you."

"Definitely not," I said as we both started to look around to see if anything had fallen.

We glanced around the living room, and everything seemed intact. Anxious fear started to dissipate and in its stead was a curious concern. We started looking under things and peering around corners. Bathrooms, hallways, around into the kitchen . . . we could see nothing that had fallen or been disturbed.

We sheepishly smiled at each other. I shrugged my shoulders, gave her a kiss, and started back toward my office. As I went to walk through the darkened dining room again, I peered toward the back wall of windows. On our deck, we'd left our IKEA folding table to the fury of winter. One thing I was struck by in that moment: There must be a clear sky and a full moon illuminating the feathers I was witnessing.

There, clinging to the edge of the table, was a huge snowy owl with wings spread almost the entire width of our dining room. Large golden eyes seemed to stare through the glass and right into me as the owl slowly brought his wings to rest at his side. I knew it was a male snowy owl because it was almost pure white. He seemed absolutely huge, illuminated there by silver moonlight. I heard Allison's tiptoes creaking on our old floor into the dining room. I knew she had followed my gaze because her breath audibly caught in her throat. At some point we must have taken each other's hands as we started to walk toward the wall of windows.

A breeze was gently rustling some of the smaller feathers on his head. At that point I realized we were within a few feet of the back windows. We were leaning forward and breathing out in deep, quiet sighs. He wasn't startled by our approach, and I realized he was probably mesmerized by the visions of his own reflection. Then he started unraveling his wings again and held himself there for the length of a sigh. Barely three or four undulations later, he was resting on a branch forty feet in the air. We craned our necks upward and looked through the glass. We didn't want Mother Nature's trance to end.

"Well, that was pretty amazing," Allison said in hushed tones.

"Yes, indeed," I said, shaking my head in wondrous disbelief.

Then we broke down into a rabble of "Are you kidding me?" and "Did that really happen?" A lot of childlike giggling and shaking our heads, and then we just held each other in a deep hug for a few minutes, aware of each other's breaths. A silent communal prayer.

A couple of months later we were cleaning up the backyard as the bits of spring started peering at us from the ground. Allison was formulating a plan about what would be planted and where. She was spending particular time on the flower versus vegetable ratio that only she knew. We wrapped fallen branches into bundles and swept the stones of the patio into a fresh seasonal clean. I scanned the yard to see what needed to be taken to the curb. The IKEA table had warped well out of its original shape. I thought it was probably something we could just leave out with the branches. As I got closer, I could see the markings—the deep wounds the talons of the great snowy owl had left in the grain of the wood. I dragged my fingers across it, and for the first time felt the shiver.

Needless to say, the table never made it to the curb. It was cleaned and found its way into my writing room and subsequent writing rooms ever since. It's held my books and music and the occasional framed photo, as well as souvenirs of Allison's and my concert tours.

My writing room today is significantly smaller and sometimes doubles as a guest room. Filling one wall is my current desk—a converted church organ from the 1800s. I get to write music on an instrument that led worship for over a hundred years. It's an amazing piece with a beautiful antique chair, and because of all of that, the room was starting to overflow. The warped IKEA table that had been scraped by silver talons had to be relegated to our basement.

In my heart I know it's safe there. That table will never make it to the curb or to Goodwill. I'll continue to unfold that memory many more times in the future. I'll drag my fingers across those markings and remember the golden gaze and windows-wide wingspan of that truly remarkable owl . . . so I can again feel that shiver.

twenty-five

Peace Eagles

GLENDA FERGUSON

The clear blue sky formed a perfect backdrop for viewing the impromptu air show. Soaring silhouettes, each with a six-foot wingspan held in a slight *V*, glided over an area of the community park. No flapping of wings was required as the group rode the warm thermals. No honks or tweets. Just silence. As I observed from the walking trail, I was reminded of the verse "Who are these that fly along like clouds?" (Isa. 60:8).

Since moving to southern Indiana two months ago, I never tired of marveling at these majestic birds. There were now half a dozen circling the park. I kept watching until the grand finale, a synchronized aerial turn. Then the group flew toward the trees along the hillside. Apparently, the roosting zone was right behind the row of houses and stores. For some reason, the birds preferred the neighborhood rather than a remote area.

Curiosity about this bird group led me to search for answers from an acquaintance who had grown up in the area. That was when I learned the impressive birds' more common names.

She replied, "Those are vultures and scavengers!"

By the disgusted look on her face, I realized she did not care at all for their flying abilities. I even regretted asking the question.

"You might admire them from far away, but don't get too close. You won't like what you see." That was how she (and I) ended the conversation.

Later I thought about her words regarding the vultures, especially the part about how I wouldn't like what I saw up close. That was exactly my fear about fitting in. I had left my hometown in Missouri to earn a master's degree in education from Indiana University. I kept even the few people I knew at a distance. Up close, they would have seen all my failures, fears, and flaws.

A week later I checked out an Audubon bird book from the library. I flipped directly to the New World turkey vultures. Their scientific name, *Cathartes aura*, roughly translated means purifier or cleansing breeze. For the first time, I saw detailed photos of a vulture's features. The red featherless head resembled a turkey. According to the book, its baldness, acute eyesight, and keen sense of smell were ideal tools for "nature's cleanup crew."

Every morning that summer at the park, I watched for the kettle of vultures. According to my research, that's what a group in flight is called, as it resembles rising bubbles in a pot of boiling water. When two or more vultures gather in trees or on fence posts, it's called a committee.

Walking on the paved trails alone gave me time to pray about my struggle to find a teaching job. I was beginning to think that my plan for my life was not God's plan for me.

To earn some money to pay for night classes, I accepted a secretarial job at the college. Meanwhile, I applied at many area schools for any elementary teaching position. One interview ended abruptly when I revealed my resignation from my last teaching position and why the school board had requested me to do so. No wonder I was not letting anyone too close. I was feeling hopeless, like a failure, but I faked a smile and an aura of confidence. I didn't wish for anyone to see the fearful me with my inferiority complex.

While planning a day trip around Indiana, I found a reference to a recreation area called Buzzard Roost. After many twists and turns, I located the site in the Hoosier National Forest. The cliffs offered spectacular bird's-eye views of the Ohio River. I saw only a few vultures, nothing like the large colonies that had been attracted to the smokehouse smells that used to permeate the area during the 1800s. From the information signage, I found out *buzzard* was the name sometimes used for the scavengers. The Cherokee called them peace eagles, because although the vultures resemble eagles at a distance, their yellowish beaks and feet aren't useful for capturing prey. From then on, that is the name I preferred.

On Sunday at church, I was on my way out the door as soon as the service ended, my usual routine. But the minister's wife called out my name. "I heard you're looking for a teaching job in the fall," she said, "but could you help out here at church now? We could really use someone to teach a group of children during Vacation Bible School."

Impulsively I replied yes. I was thinking this was an opportunity to get my mind off myself and focused on helping others.

I picked up the packaged teaching materials, which were based on the theme: "But those who hope in the LORD will renew their strength. They will soar on wings like eagles; they will run and not grow weary, they will walk and not be faint" (Isa. 40:31). The children and I discussed how an eagle appears in flight. I was able to tell them how other birds with large wingspans soar, taking advantage of the warm air to gain higher altitudes.

I learned right along with the children about hope, about gaining strength through God and not giving up on your dreams. At the end of the week, I felt renewed and ready to soar, not like a lone eagle but more like the peace eagles.

I started staying after church for Bible study with a small group. Occasionally, I opened up about the stress I'd experienced since moving away from home. The church community encouraged me and included me in many activities.

In the fall, I was hired as a teacher's aide in first grade. I thought it was because of my resume and experience. But several teachers at church had seen how I interacted with the children at VBS and recommended me to the school administration. After that year, I was hired in other temporary teaching positions and later hired full-time at a nearby school.

Recently I found this quote: "Birds that fly high never concern themselves about crossing streams."[3] Perhaps that quote and my story might help others see their struggles from another angle, not from a worldly view but from heaven's view. There are not many people who can say they were inspired by turkey vultures. But I was. Perhaps it just sounds better to say I gained inspiration from a church community and the peace eagles.

twenty-six

A Bird's-Eye View

LYNN DOVE

I suppose when I married into the Dove family, I could have expected that birds (especially doves) would somehow have a special place in my life. When I was a child in the mid-sixties, my parents inherited an Amazonian parrot that we affectionately called Gomer. We inherited this bird after we befriended some sailors from a Danish freighter that had run into another freighter just off the west coast of Vancouver Island. The call went out to all Danish-speaking citizens in the Victoria area to host these sailors while their ship was undergoing repairs. My parents answered the call, and for several weeks we became the adopted family to three burly Danish sailors who had the most colorful tattoos I had ever seen and the most colorful Danish language too! They spent their time with us eating—a lot—(did I mention they were burly?) and watching wrestling matches on our TV.

One day they showed up with Gomer after the cook on their ship had taken a vicious dislike to the birds squawking all day at him while he was preparing the onboard meals. He had already dispatched Gomer's mate with a butcher knife and was threatening to behead Gomer before the sailors rescued him. We quickly discovered that Gomer's squawking was definitely something to get used to, but my mother had endless patience with the bird and eventually trained him to speak several polite English words and not to repeat the "colorful" words he had learned while on board the Danish ship. (No doubt he must have learned some of those words from the cook brandishing a butcher knife. Haha.)

Gomer became part of our family, and one day we discovered that he had a penchant for red wine after my cousin mistakenly allowed Gomer to lick what we thought was red cherry soda from his fingers after a family dinner. We only discovered the mistake when the bird hung upside down in his cage for an hour and sang Danish drinking songs before keeling off his perch to sleep off the hangover.

My next brush with feathers was the summer my daughter (a middle-schooler then) begged me to look after the school's two cockatiels. (I should have remembered what happened the summer we looked after the preschool's hamster, but that's another story.) The two birds shared a huge cage together and between the two of them kicked out enough feathers to fill a king-size duvet! They didn't much like people, or at least me, because every time I went near the cage to clean it or give them food or water, they attacked my outstretched arms and fingers with vigor. I made the mistake of not closing the latch on the cage door properly one day, and we spent hours chasing them around the house while they dive-bombed and pooped on us as they flew past. (I seriously considered getting out my butcher knife!)

Several summers ago, while camping with my family, I witnessed a "bird drama" unfold on Mirror Lake near Kaslo, British Columbia. The lake is home to a family of ducks, but this particular summer a confused Canada goose had somehow been adopted by the ducks. When they quacked, he honked! When they waddled up to the campsites to beg for food from campers, the goose followed along contentedly. For days I watched as the ducks and goose interacted. They certainly seemed to have a special camaraderie.

One morning, a gaggle of geese descended with great trumpeting and fanfare onto the lake. Ducks scattered as the great geese splashed down and honked noisily to each other. It only took minutes for the other geese to notice the lone goose amongst his duck buddies. I don't speak "goose," but it was pretty obvious that the gist of the conversation took the form of "goose bullying."

"Are you kidding me? Whatcha doing hangin' around with those ducks?" Pretty soon the lone goose, feeling shamed, I suppose, left his duck friends to swim with his new goose posse. Minutes later, I watched in amazement as the geese lifted off with great cacophony, and with a final splash goodbye to his duck friends, the lone goose joined his new friends in the sky. They circled the lake once and then headed south, and I did not see them again. I have often wondered if the ducks missed the goose or vice versa.

For the longest time, I was sure that birds were totally incapable of showing any kind of human emotion until I witnessed a bird drama that would rival the angst of Romeo and Juliet. Two blackbirds, a male and a female, were chasing each other noisily around the house. I knew this because whenever our dog, Samson, saw a bird outside, he would chase them from one window to the next from inside the house, barking madly at them the whole time. This time, though, his barking stopped abruptly when the female bird banged off a back window and landed with a thud on our deck. I knew the sound; birds sometimes careen into those windows, and the outcome is much the same each time. They usually don't survive. Sure enough, the little bird's neck was broken.

I am always saddened when something like that happens, but sometimes animals and civilization collide. I knew that by day's end, a fox, coyote, or hawk would take the carcass of the bird as an easy meal. It was nature's way. I shooed Samson from the window, but then I noticed a heartbreaking scene unfold. The male mate of the deceased bird was pacing beside the body. A few times he would lift off and circle and then light back down and pace again. He flew off and was gone several minutes, and when I looked again, he had a worm in his beak and was trying to feed the worm to his mate, in hopes it would somehow revive her.

I had never thought birds could "love" one another, but it was obvious that I was witnessing a great display of affection here. When the male realized that his beloved was gone, he left the worm like a farewell offering and flew off. As I'd known would happen, sometime over the course of the next few hours, while I was not watching, the carcass of the bird was mysteriously removed from the deck by either a bird of prey or by some other scavenger.

Now, you might think that is the end to the bird drama, but the next morning I noticed a little blackbird through our skylight, collecting and dropping rocks on our sloped roof. Though the rocks were small, they made enough noise as they skipped along the roof shakes to catch my attention. It was obvious that the little male bird was trying to enact some kind of revenge on the monster (our house) that he perceived had murdered his mate. Like a little "Rambo," he attacked with vengeance. I can't help but think that every time he dropped a rock on our roof, he was thinking, *Take that, Monster! This one is for the missus!*

I find it interesting that Scripture mentions birds (ravens, sparrows, eagles, doves, etc.), not to teach us about them, but to convey lessons learned from watching those birds. For example, the Bible mentions the eagle twenty-eight times. Twenty-six of those times the eagle teaches some kind of lesson.

Job 12:7–12 says, "But ask the animals, and they will teach you, or the birds in the sky, and they will tell you; or speak to the earth, and it will teach you, or let the fish in the sea inform you. Which of all these does not know that the hand of the Lord has done this? In his hand is the life of every creature and the breath of all mankind. Does not the ear test words as the tongue tastes food? Is not wisdom found among the aged? Does not long life bring understanding?"

Scripture says that God watches over each one of his creation, including sparrows (Matt. 10:29–31). The Greek word used is the diminutive form of the word for sparrow, thus, "little sparrows." The idea here is that if God watches over the tiniest of birds and even knows when one falls from the sky, how much more is he aware of his children who are "worth more than many sparrows" (v. 31).

I once heard it said that there is never a sparrow dies but that God goes to its funeral. How tender-spirited is the Lord, that he cares so much for the smallest of birds? Did the tears well up in his eyes, as they did in mine, when he watched the blackbird mourn the loss of his mate? Does God care that much for a bird? Scripture says he does! How much more does he love me, a "Dove" by name, a bird-watcher at times, "bird-brained" occasionally, but mostly just an ordinary woman journeying through life daily with God?

I am constantly encouraged that God has a "bird's-eye view" of me!

twenty-seven

Tillman–The Payback Bird

SHERRY DIANE KITTS

As a child, I enjoyed all kinds of pets. Most of the time, my parents helped me choose them. One day I asked Dad for fifty cents.

"Why do you need fifty cents?" he asked.

"It's a surprise."

"Okay. I don't think fifty cents can cause much damage."

Within a few minutes I ran into our kitchen carrying a small brown box and glowing with glee.

"Surprise!" I opened the top. "It's a hamster! I bought it from my friend Carol."

"Yes. It is a hamster," my dad said.

Dad never gave me money again without knowing the purpose of my request.

During my teen years, an unexpected gift arrived when my boyfriend, Rich, carried in another surprise. Rich set the box by the front door. He lifted the flaps, and we peered inside. A fluffy white rabbit with neon pink eyes stared back. My parents raised their brows at each other, then at me. I understood that look. I wanted to win their approval of the little cottontail bunny and began commenting on his clean and healthy condition.

My boyfriend straightened his shoulders and raised his chin. "I got him at the feed-and-seed store downtown."

"He is cute," Mom said.

I seized the moment. "Let's call him Clarence."

The corners of Dad's mouth turned into a slight smile as he spoke to my boyfriend. "One day you'll get payback."

I wasn't sure what he meant or what the payback might be. I brushed it off when Dad agreed to build a cage to keep Clarence comfortable and safe.

Accelerate many years forward to my marriage with Rich and to our own daughter's teen years.

One evening our daughter's boyfriend came by with a special gift. She called us to the hallway to see it. Inside a cage on a little perch sat the unexpected "payback."

A cockatiel.

The tables had now turned, and I looked at the cockatiel and then over to my husband, Rich. He glared at the bird. I could picture his thoughts moving across his forehead like a flashing sign: *What in the world are we going to do with that?* But Renee's smiles and her expression of "Can I keep him?" prompted Rich to let this one slide.

Rich accepted the cockatiel into our home.

"But with one rule," he said. "You're going to take care of this bird."

The cockatiel's coloring captivated my attention. His gray body had white flashes on the outer edge of each wing. He had a yellow head and an outstanding crest that popped up and down as he moved. Bright orange circles highlighted each side of his face like he was decked out for a circus show. We made a place in the living room for the cockatiel and named him Tillman. The

German origin of the name means "ruler of people." At times, we thought Mr. Tillman embodied that name.

We had much to learn about cockatiels.

During his first days with us, Tillman settled into our home and munched his seeds with contentment. When we walked by him, he'd bob his head and tilt his tufted crown. He seemed delightful. An attractive addition.

Renee decided to pet him and poked her finger through the cage.

"Ow! He bit me!"

"He didn't try to bite you. He just gave a friendly peck. Let me show you." I eased my finger through his cage to touch his head. With dramatic speed, he turned his head and clamped his beak points into my index finger. I yanked back my finger, hitting one of the wires and rocking his cage.

"Wow! So much for petting him. Let's give him time to get used to us and settle into his new surroundings."

"I'm not sure time will help," Renee said.

The bird's response to our affectionate attempts turned us away from close encounters.

We were accustomed to daybreak melodies of birds in our yard, but not to Tillman's screeches as he greeted the sunrise. His early reveille pierced everyone's mornings. Weekends were no exception. Our initial delight with him soon wore away.

"Is there anything to help hush this bird in the morning?" Rich said.

Back in those days, Google didn't exist for problem solving. I called my mother.

"Mom, Tillman's high-pitched screeches are too much. What can I do?"

"Put a cover over his cage at night. He'll know it's time to rest, and then you can uncover it in the morning when everyone's awake."

"Thanks. Good idea."

The cover did help at night, but in the morning, Tillman let everyone know he didn't agree with sleeping in. If you didn't uncover him early, he'd repeat his warble or release a long wolf whistle. During the day, napping was short for this chatty cockatiel, and even then, you could hear him chirping.

One summer, Rich's mother agreed to keep the bird while we went on a week's vacation. We cleaned his cage and readied all his food supplies. Nana lived alone and welcomed our bird's company. When we returned to get Tillman, she said she'd be sad to see him go. We looked at each other in shock.

"I'm sorry, Nana, if Tillman's screeching kept you awake," Renee said.

"Oh, he didn't bother me. I talked to him whenever I sat in the TV room. I taught him to say a few things."

"What? I've never heard him say anything," I said.

Nana walked to his cage. "Hello, hello."

Tillman looked at us and then at Nana. He nodded and said, "Hello."

Our jaws fell open.

"See, I told you," Nana said to us. She turned toward Tillman again. "Pretty boy. Pretty boy."

He tilted his head from side to side, sat tall on his perch, and lifted his crest.

"Pretty boy," he repeated. If a bird ever looked proud of himself, Tillman did.

Nana smiled and said, "You just have to talk to him. He loves conversation."

Why didn't we see that Tillman wanted to talk with us? We reasoned that our lack of communication hinged on a busy schedule. Renee's days were filled with finishing high school and socializing, and I began working a full-time job. From the beginning,

Rich expressed his position that he would be uninvolved in the bird's care.

After we witnessed Nana's success with our cockatiel, we wanted to achieve the same rapport she shared with Tillman. He was a beautiful bird who craved attention. She took the time to notice him and to engage in conversation. We began to recognize his moods. We talked with him more and offered toys and treats. As time progressed, Tillman even welcomed a gentle rub on his head. He seemed happy to be included in our family.

Tillman grew more acclimated to our home. Renee and her boyfriend decided he may enjoy getting out of the cage. He did like it. So much so that he didn't want to return. When they tried to gather him in their hands, he flew erratically from curtain rods, to the dresser, to picture frames.

"Mom! We can't get Tillman in his cage." She knew his sharp beak could still deliver a painful peck.

"I'm coming. I'll wear gloves and bring a towel."

I tiptoed into the bedroom.

I tried to use a reassuring voice. "It's okay, Tillie bird. It's okay."

He'd landed on the bed's headboard. I tossed the towel over the cockatiel and gently scooped him up.

I put him back inside the cage, and his little chest palpated as he recovered from the flight escapade. We decided to let him remain there. I think Tillman agreed.

The day came for Renee to graduate and move on to college. My husband gave her the same notice my father had given me about my rabbit when I left for college.

"You have to find somewhere for Tillman to go. We can't keep caring for him while you're away."

One of the ladies I worked with had parrots and a few other birds. I told her about our cockatiel and asked if she'd welcome him into her home aviary. After consulting her husband, she said yes. We packed Tillman's belongings and loaded him inside his cage into the car. When we arrived, Tillman seemed glad to be greeted by the other birds all chirping and warbling their own tunes. He chimed in with his usual screeches. On the ride home we shed a few tears. We knew we'd miss our crazy bird.

Renee left for school, and I continued working. Tillman's new owner said Tillman had adjusted well and enjoyed his association with her other birds. After Tillman's time with us, we realized we shouldn't put a cover over life's challenges and walk away. Benefits abound when we pause to communicate and notice each other. Sometimes we applaud another's successes. Sometimes we crave a hug when the day has been unkind. Sometimes we forgive when another's voice is too shrill or sharp.

Tillman, the cockatiel, arrived as a payback gift and left as a pay-it-forward gift. We became aware of our needs to talk with each other, to listen, and to care.

twenty-eight

Rockin' Rosa

MAUREEN M. ELWYN

Squinting from the glare of the bright sunlight flooding the breakfast nook, I tiptoed to the window to peer through the pane at
the nest a mere three feet away. Much to my delight, three baby
robins turned their heads to stare back at me, totally uncon-
cerned by my presence. By now, my frequent visits had become
a constant occurrence in their day and served no threat to their
existence. Joining me with a coffee cup in hand, my husband,
Paul, surveyed the scene and murmured, "And to think she built
that nest on top of a rock!"

Earlier in the month, their mother had decided to construct
her nest on the electric meter situated a mere stone's throw from
our kitchen window. Believing she would be much safer (not
to mention less messy), Paul and I tried every way we could to
discourage the robin, but the nesting urge is stronger than human
common sense, and nothing we did dampened the enthusiasm
of the determined bird.

When she first started fashioning a nest from the dried grass and strings she picked up in the yard, Paul slipped out and threw them on the ground, thinking she would surely take the hint and build on the tree limb that almost touched the meter. Each time, she seemed to understand the point we were trying to make and disappeared for the rest of the day. A quick peek outside the following morning, however, found her once again building a firm foundation, an action she would repeat for the next three days, the pattern never changing: Robin builds. Humans tear down.

Equally resolute, I recommended a different strategy and suggested that Paul scour the driveway for some big rocks. After a brief search, he found a pointed rock that perfectly fit the tiny space on top of the meter and added a couple of smaller rocks on the other side of the pole for good measure. "That ought to do it!" I exclaimed, confident that we had reached the perfect solution, but alas, it was not to be so. Midmorning revealed the bird scrunched in between the rock and the hard metal pole. I swear she gave me a haughty glare when I looked out the window. We were totally at a loss, outwitted by our fine feathered friend.

Unfortunately, a family illness forced us to leave home for a week. On the drive home, I wondered aloud if we would discover a nest upon our return. As soon as the suitcases were deposited in our bedroom, I ran to the kitchen window, gazing out in the deepening twilight. Much to my amazement, I saw not just a nest but what Paul and I would later dub a two-story robin condominium. Perched on top sat one very proud bird.

I named her Rosa. After all, we were next-door neighbors now. Paul took her picture from behind the screen so we wouldn't disturb her, thus allowing her to devote her time and energy to motherhood. Two days later when our daughter came to visit, I asked her to peruse the domicile while Rosa took a few minutes to stretch her wings, which were surely tired and cramped from the close quarters in which she was living. Much to our delight, three beautiful blue eggs graced the nursery. No longer annoyed, we were elated—awed at the wonder of a tiny creature so insistent on creating her dream home in the exact location she had selected.

Unfortunately, another out-of-state trip called us away from home again the next week, and this time when we returned home, three baby birds stretched their necks above the top of the nest as Rosa fed them worms she found in our yard.

In the Sermon on the Mount, Jesus tells the story of two men who built houses. One chose to build his house on the shifting sands, but the wiser of the two constructed his house on a rock. When the rains came down and the floods came up, the house on the sand (according to the children's song) went SPLAT! The house built on the rock, on the other hand, stayed firm.

Leave it to a little bird to remind me of an important truth. Try as we would to deter her, Rosa knew exactly what she was doing when she built her nest on top of the pointed rock that we had placed on the electric meter. The rains came and the winds blew, but her little house withstood whatever came her way. If I will just follow her example and anchor my life to the Rock, I, too, can be assured that my foundation will remain unshakable.

Thanks, Rosa, for moving in next door. I hope you will stay a long time.

twenty-nine

The Golden Girls
and the New Brood

DJ PERRY

"Thank you for being a friend. Travel down the road and back again." These lyrics open the TV show *The Golden Girls*, and they just so happen to play into my story. So, let's just start our tale with . . .

Once upon a time in the mitten state of Michigan, there was a large cultivated space in our backyard that had been dedicated to growing produce. The handheld tiller worked the soil all while giving me some version of a Mr. Miyagi/Karate Kid workout. The twisting and turning of the dirt took a good hour and change. Some things grew great in the garden space, like tomatoes and green beans. Other plants, like the onions, cabbage, and pumpkins, did not fare as well. A few more seasons of the 1800s-style ground prepping drove me to acquire a gas-powered tiller. So efficient was this new gadget that I completed my tilling job in a solid ten minutes. But alas, I still had plenty of back-breaking work to do—daily weeding or picking of beans and such. It all seemed to wear on an aging back. Even with the new tools, gardening was easier but not easy.

Not long after one of our yearly 4-H trips, my better half brought up the topic of chickens. I thought she was expressing a newfound interest, a possible new hobby, and I wanted to be supportive. We had several such discussions about chickens, and I was getting all kinds of questions lobbed my way. How many would be ideal? What breed of chickens? What size coop? Where should a coop go? My response was basically of the "whatever you want" variety. Breeds? Coops? I had no idea. Since the chickens were going to be her chickens, her responsibility, I was fine with however she wanted the setup. She quickly stated that she had thought *I* wanted the chickens. I already make wine and beer. I play soccer and the guitar and enjoy my occasional archery. I stated firmly that I had enough hobbies and was just trying to be supportive. So that put an end to the discussion. Or did it?

A few weeks later, the subject came back up again over Sunday coffee. She told me about chicken breeds best suited for certain climates. Really? She informed me that chicken coops had to be X distance from a property line. Interesting facts. I learned that no roosters were allowed in the city limits. I nodded right along. Long story short, someone had to finally admit that *she* wanted to start raising chickens. It was a rare moment indeed. I felt like I had won something, somehow. When asked again about my thoughts, I told her that I could tell how bad she really wanted them. I pondered for a few moments before exclaiming that the garden area was the best place to put the coop. She wholeheartedly agreed. I saw that my days of picking beans were almost at an end.

A farm supply store sourced our first coop, and a nearby farm our first residents. That was when Blanche, Rose, Dorothy, and

147

Sophia, the Golden Girls, came to live with us. We also ended up getting two raised beds for the veggies. They could now be harvested while standing. Brilliant!

We quickly learned that our Golden Girls had to have a certain wing clipped if we did not want them flying off. One that did fly out of the enclosure was quickly tackled by Finn, our boxer/pit bull mix. Think Snoopy on steroids. He was content to hold her down and pull out several tail feathers, like a game of she-loves-me, she-loves-me-not. Other than ending up a bit light on feathers, our escapee was not harmed in the encounter.

More trips to the farm store to get mealworms, water dispensers, straw, calcium, scratch feed, and coop heaters to use on a cold Michigan night. So much goes into this chicken hobby. If you took all the expenses and divided it by the number of eggs, our eggs only cost us $100 or so a dozen. No, an egg. Okay, maybe not that bad, but we're not saving a great amount by raising chickens. But it's not about the eggs, I'm told. It's about the chickens.

The chicken lovers will tell you the birds have little personalities akin to a dog. They get excited to see you and run to greet you. Their awkward gait and strut are reminiscent of the raptors in *Jurassic Park* as they stalk every little creature be it worm, grub, bug, or even once a wild baby bird. I still stand by the assessment that if chickens were six to seven feet tall, they would eat us all.

The miracle that is egg laying started a short time after we got the girls, and we found ourselves with an abundance of eggs. Not just any eggs but the freshest eggs. Often still warm and with a rich color inside and out.

But back to the dog comparison. I already have a huge, soft heart that grieves greatly the loss of any of our pets. I wasn't sure that I wanted to form a bond like that with the chickens. I thought that if allowed to, they would domesticate more like a dog into our lives. I had a friend in Maggie Valley, North Carolina, who kept a little rooster, Samson, in the house, roosting in the closet. He roamed freely, played with the cat daily, and was just one of the many critters living in that household. I did not need that with the Golden Girls. They had their own space outside, and I had mine.

It's now a good many years later, and the Golden Girls have all passed on, much like the TV actresses. But "Chicken Land" has continued to grow with the addition of a much larger and more insulated Amish-built coop. The chickens still use the older "Community Coop" for daytime hanging. But the larger, heavy-duty coop is so well built, a human could sleep in it. Good information to know should one get in trouble and the doghouse is already taken. The area now has planted herbs and blueberries, all stuff they love to eat. Clover, a chicken treat, now covers the lawn. The many stumps and decaying leaves create excellent hunting grounds for a chicken seeking worms or grubs.

Our yard has been turned into a chicken paradise, if you will. And with the current cost of eggs, having your own supply is a nice luxury. For a few months following the hens' molting, egg production stops. I hear that it all has to do with the amount of daylight. As soon as spring starts to return, the eggs start appearing again. (I want to credit the return to production to my daily humorous threats to host a chicken BBQ if egg production does not resume.) I'm happy to report that as of yesterday, we're back to full production. For us, that's one egg per chicken, per day.

I never thought I would be a chicken farmer, but I guess maybe I am. So Old Mc DJ had a farm, E-I-E-I-O, and on our farm, we had some chickens, E-I-E-I-O. I want to thank our original Golden Girls, who started us on this path. Thank you for being our first brood, flock, clutch, collection, peep, flight, or run of birds. And thank you for being a friend.

thirty

No Paparazzi Allowed

WENDY KLOPFENSTEIN

"Girls! Come look." Mom's excited call came from the French doors by the back patio.

Her tone meant one thing. She'd spotted wildlife, most likely a bird, on our five-acre plot in central Oklahoma. My sister, Danielle, and I rushed to glimpse Mom's new find. A roadrunner. There he stood by the back corner of the fence where our property backed up to the cow pasture, which stretched as far as you could see. The crest of feathers atop his head moved with all the jerky movements of the famous cartoon character, the one forever chased by a coyote. While we had plenty of coyotes running across our property every night, we'd yet to see their counterpart. Until now.

"Quick. Get the camera." I made a shooing motion with my hand to my sister.

Since cameras weren't yet in every cell phone, she had to locate the one usually stashed in the living room cabinets. By the time Danielle returned, our new friend had run off with all the speed we'd expected from a roadrunner. Much to our delight, that day wasn't our only sighting. It was the beginning of a unique relationship. Neighbors sharing the same space.

Our very own roadrunner began to make regular appearances. His presence delighted us. Never afraid to make his presence known, he took to tapping at the back door glass. The first time I heard it, I called to the others as I approached in amazement. We gathered at the back door, his willing audience. Legs and a long green tail poked out from the corners of his beak as he proudly showed off the lizard he'd caught. With a side-to-side jerking motion, he moved his head so we could get a good view. Had he brought his breakfast by to show us? Or was this the universal sign of friendship—an invitation to a meal? He was in no rush to leave until one of us approached with the camera. At the first sight of the lens, he sped away to disappear behind a retaining wall of railroad ties.

Trying to take his picture became a sort of game. A game he seemed to enjoy. He'd announce his arrival via a tap on the glass or a prancing in front of the windows by the front flower beds. Then, the minute one of us attempted to aim a lens in his direction, he ran with all the speed his legs possessed. His aversion to the camera was a puzzle I never understood. What about the large black object in front of our faces did he object to?

My sister and I devised a plan to capture the likeness of this camera-shy bird. The next time we saw him, one of us would remain standing in his sight at the window, while the other snuck around outside to snap his photo. That way, we reasoned, he wouldn't suspect a camera coming his way. It sounded like the perfect idea.

A few days later, I spotted him out the front window. With hand signals on the scale of a SWAT team maneuver, Danielle and I communicated. She stood by the door, pointing at the camera, while I signaled for her to go. Danielle slipped out the back door as silently as possible with the camera hanging from the strap around her neck. As I stood tracking the movements of the roadrunner, he moved toward the side of the house. Perfect. His path would take him right to the spot where Danielle stood, camera at the ready. Or so I imagined.

I watched for any signs of him coming back in my direction as I waited with anticipation. When she was no longer in my line of sight, I pictured Danielle getting the perfect photo as he sauntered around the corner of the house unawares. A yelp sounded from outside. Alarm ran through me. Had the roadrunner suddenly become aggressive? He'd always appeared friendly, but we were dealing with wildlife. With a long beak and claws, he could be capable of harming us. I rushed to the door, only to collide with my sister as she hurried back into the house.

"What happened?"

She strained to catch her breath while the camera hung limp. "He surprised me."

"He surprised you?" Wasn't it supposed to be the other way around?

"I moved around the side of the house. As I rounded the corner, we were face to face." Her breaths came in short bursts. "I was so surprised, I yelped."

"Did you get a photo?" This was perfect. Up close and personal.

"No. He ran away as soon as I raised the camera."

Foiled again. Obviously, this roadrunner did not want his picture taken.

One day, Mom called from the back door again. "Girls! Come look at this."

Gathered by the glass, we saw it. Two roadrunners graced our backyard. Our friend had brought his mate to meet us. While she waited in the distance, he approached the door. It was as if he were asking, "What do you think of her?"

We grinned and waved our approval. After that, his visits grew less frequent. Maybe his mate preferred to nest away from prying human eyes. While he had hung around the property for over a year, maybe even two, we were never able to capture a good photo of him. In the distance, no problem. With his back turned, fleeing, sure. But up close, no way. How were we supposed to convince anyone we had a friendly, approachable roadrunner who made regular visits without proof? Would anyone believe he liked to come peck on the door to show off his dinner to us? Finally, we decided it didn't matter.

We were given a rare gift of an unusual sort of friendship with this roadrunner. In later years, we'd occasionally catch sight of a roadrunner on the property at a distance. Was it our old friend? Or one of his offspring? We like to think so. And while he may not have been the famous roadrunner from the cartoons, he always made one thing clear: No paparazzi allowed.

thirty-one

A Little Bit of Fluff

LAURAINE SNELLING

I was so excited that summer Saturday, cleaning house because my husband Wayne's sister and family were coming to visit. Our cockatiel Bidley was perched on my shoulder, one of his favorite places. I'd thought I wanted a parrot in those years but was so glad we got a cockatiel instead. Our kids were trying to teach him to talk but not having a lot of success. He talked plenty in his own language and made us laugh. Then he would bob his head as if taking a bow.

We'd made dessert, a gingerbread cake from scratch, which was now cooling on the counter to be served with cream yet to be whipped. Lemonade and iced tea cooled in the refrigerator. Daughter Marie was sweeping the carport, sons Brian and Kevin were mowing and raking the front yard. This was our relatives' first visit in years, since they lived in Kansas. They were driving a rental RV, and from our house in Vancouver, Washington, they would head north to the Olympic National Forest on the Olympic Peninsula.

Have I mentioned we were all excited? Marie to help her two young cousins ride her horse Cimmaron, Kevin to introduce them to his pigs, and Brian hoping they'd get to see his banty rooster and hen. Bidley always got excited when anyone else was. I think he picked up the vibes.

Last thing to be done was shaking out the rugs. I scooped them up and took them out the back door.

I felt Bidley's wings as he flew off my shoulder.

We all called and called, because Bidley usually answered us. We stood under our big fir tree right off the back door, checking all the branches, and inspected all the shrubbery around our house. Our little bird had gotten out once before, and we'd gotten him down from the roof. But now, no answering. No bright flashes of green or yellow.

Where had he gone?

Our company came, the girls enjoyed their rides, but using a stick to scratch the pigs did not seem a good idea, and everyone chuckled at the chickens. We ate our dessert, chatting all the while. Bidley would have loved the visit from the safety of my shoulder. He was always a bit shy with new people. I kept praying God would bring our little bird back.

We waved our visitors on their way and went back to searching, now beyond our acre. Prayers continued that God would bring Bidley back to us. I reminded myself it was summer, so he would be comfortable, not shivering against some tree trunk. We had plenty of woods in our area.

Dinner that night was pretty quiet, with my family sending me it's-all-your-fault-Mom glances. At least that's what I thought they were saying. Guilt raised its ugly head. Indeed, I was at fault.

Life went on as life does. I started writing, hoping at the time for publication. The kids graduated and went on to college and drafting school, Wayne and I moved to California for a new job for him, and we learned what living in an apartment was like. Son Brian gave us another cockatiel, and years passed, busy as always.

Our family, now only four of us since Marie died from cancer, gathered together to celebrate a holiday, something we didn't get to do very often because we lived so far apart. We were happily reminiscing when Kevin said, "Mom, remember Bidley?"

I nodded and sighed. "Of course."

"There was a happy ending."

We all stared at him.

"You remember that group of houses west of us, say half a mile or so?"

"Sure. We drove by them plenty of times."

"I was talking with a friend of mine about living there, and he said, 'You guys had a cockatiel, right?' I agreed, and he told me that a relative of his lived in one of those houses and had the craziest thing happen. They saw a little bird in their yard, a cockatiel of all things."

"You've got to be kidding!"

"Nope, they put a birdcage out on the lawn and watched from the window as that little bird climbed into the cage and started eating right away."

I sniffed. I cry easily. "Someone found him, and he didn't get eaten by a hawk or something."

"They tried to find out who lost their cockatiel but couldn't, so they kept him and said he made their lives richer."

"So I guess our prayers were answered after all."

Funny, but thanks to that dear little bit of fluff, I learned about praying unceasingly. The song so often running through my mind? "My God is so great, so strong and so mighty, there's nothing my God cannot do."

thirty-two

Lindy Says Hello

LEE JUSLIN

Lindy, a double yellow-headed Panama parrot, was given to my mother by her father around the time Lindbergh made his historic flight. So, of course, she named him Lindy.

Lindy was well established in the family before my arrival. However, since parrots live almost as long as humans, he was a teenager and still pretty active when I was born.

Lindy resided in a tall brass and metal cage that would probably be considered a decorative antique today. There was a brass base on the floor with a pipe that extended up about four feet to an oval metal base. The top part was brass with a ring at the very top. Inside there was a perch extending end to end with two iron cups that screwed into either end. One held water and the other seed. At the top was a swing. He would hang from the swing and dip his head into his water dish while flapping his wings. This was his way of taking a bath.

Cleaning the cage was not easy. My mother spread newspaper on a table in the kitchen, lifted the top of the cage, and carried it out to the kitchen while Lindy held on to one side. I never understood why he didn't just drop out. Sometimes my mother's arm grew tired and rested on the bars. These were the times Lindy lived for. Always on guard, he would reach up and bite her arm with his big, curved bill. Those bites always left a large black and blue mark. And, while it hurt, my mother never held it against him, or at least not for long.

Lindy's vocabulary was not large. My mother taught him to say "firecracker" when offered a treat. She felt "Polly wants a cracker" was too common, so somehow she came up with firecracker.

Lindy's proudest vocabulary accomplishment was "hello," which he said in a number of different voices and not always to greet someone. He could say it very softly or scream out "Helloooo!" He also had a number of voices in between.

Lindy often escaped his cage by chewing through the metal base, making a hole where he could squeeze out. When this happened, my mother would put him in his smaller cage she referred to as his traveling cage and take the big base down to a local auto body shop where they would weld the hole closed. I often wondered what they told their families at dinner about their welding work that day.

When I was in grade school, we went on vacation to Niagara Falls, which was where my father was from. We stayed with his brother's family in a cottage on the Canadian side. Lindy boarded at the local pet shop. Looking at this from an adult point of view, I'm sure he was not happy. Parrots like to be with their people. They don't enjoy being alone.

Lindy's life definitely looked up when my parents bought a lot at the Jersey Shore on Long Beach Island. When I was in ninth grade, my parents and I went to a land auction to bid on various lots. There were a lot of developers outbidding us, but eventually these professionals took pity on us, and my father bought a lot on 13th Street. After securing the land parcel, my father hired a builder for a cottage.

The builder said our cottage would be ready July Fourth weekend. Taking this as a firm date, we packed up the station wagon, ready to move in to our new cottage. We always had a station wagon. My father viewed them as the perfect family car. This one had a third seat, which had been removed for cargo. A roof rack had been added for additional boxes. No doubt looking like the Beverly Hillbillies, my parents sat in front and I sat in the second seat with our dog and Lindy in his traveling cage.

Lindy had never gone for a long car ride. When he boarded at the pet shop, the trip was no more than a mile. But the ride to the cottage, or "down the shore," as we say in New Jersey, was a two-and-a-half-hour ride.

Lindy sat quietly in his cage and proved to be a good traveler except for one incident. When the dog fell asleep, one paw fell over to the edge of Lindy's cage. No one noticed because I had fallen asleep, and my mother was nodding off too. In the quiet, Lindy slipped over and bit the dog's paw. Suddenly there was a loud scream from the dog, some choice swear words from my father, and the car veered sharply to the left. Fortunately, there was little traffic, and my father was able to right the ship. When I looked at him, Lindy seemed to have a twinkle in his eye. The rest of the trip was uneventful.

When we pulled into the cottage front yard, it was clear that the July Fourth date had been an estimate. There was no front door, only a screen door. The floors were not finished, and no window screens had been installed.

The furniture my mother had ordered had not yet been delivered, so we used folding chairs to sit on. Luckily my mother did have an old table to set Lindy's cage on.

At first the workers didn't notice Lindy. However, he couldn't stay silent for long, and pretty soon he was muttering and chortling. One after another, the workers came to see what kind of bird we had. Several said he was the largest parakeet they had ever seen. My mother explained he was a parrot from Panama. When the workers quit for the day, many were talking about Lindy.

The next morning, I awoke to parrot sounds and human laughter. The workers were gathered around Lindy's cage, offering him screwdrivers and other tools. Lindy was obligingly lunging at each offering, and the workers were laughing and elbowing each other.

When the workers went back to their jobs, a small boy appeared at the door, came in, and cautiously approached Lindy. He asked what it was, and my mother again explained that Lindy was a parrot.

Soon, a woman approached, screaming for Timmy. The boy, obviously the missing Timmy, paid no attention. The woman came in, introduced herself as a neighbor in the next block, grabbed Timmy, and left.

My mother and I looked at each other, knowing what would come next. And sure enough, over the next few days, a variety of children knocked on our door and asked if this was where the big bird lived. The same thing had happened back at home, giving me quite a bit of street cred and a good subject for required essays.

Lindy continued to be a source of curiosity at the cottage. He demanded attention by calling out when he wanted a head scratch or just someone to notice him. He developed a new trick to get the attention of visitors. Sitting in his cage next to one end of the sofa, he would slip down and firmly dump his water dish on the person unlucky enough to be sitting on that end of the sofa.

As time went on and I graduated college and was living and working on my own, it became difficult for my mother to tend to Lindy. I was not in a position to take him. So, reluctantly, my mother found a sanctuary for parrots and other birds and placed him there so he could live out his final years with feathered friends and caretakers to give him the attention he craved.

thirty-three

Never Underestimate
a Bird Brain

JENNY LYNN KELLER

Most houseguests behave well, clean up any mess they make, and leave within a short period of time. Not mine, so please allow me to rant about them for a few moments. I never invited this couple to my house, and I asked them to leave multiple times. When they didn't, I pursued numerous ways to evict them in a polite and compassionate manner. They responded by taking over more of my house. To prevent the same frustrating events happening to you, please heed my warning and never underestimate a bird brain. A pair of eastern phoebes outsmarted me and now occupy my home.

After years of matching wits with the feisty couple, here's my advice. Don't be fooled by the cute little bundle of feathers sitting on a tree limb and singing a lovely melody. Ignore the fact eastern phoebes reduce the number of pesky flying insects around your house. Be aware that renowned researchers confirm that the brownish gray-and-white flycatchers rate higher on the intelligence scale than you think. Along with other songbirds, phoebes possess more brain cells per volume than some mammals. If you think I'm joking, look up "bird brain" on your favorite internet search engine. I learned about their cleverness the hard way.

We had built our dream house in the woods and enjoyed the solitude for several years before the fine-feathered squatters arrived. Then one spring I noticed a small, dark-colored bird building a nest on the backside of our garage under the overhang. Weeks later I observed two birds flying in and out of the same location but thought nothing more about them since we rarely ventured to that area.

A year later I discovered a new bird nest on the opposite end of the garage. Not long afterward, I spotted a pair of the same type of birds flying into the new nest. Like any curious bird lover, I retrieved my bird book and identified our houseguests as eastern phoebes. Their husky "phoebe" call and distinctive tail wag make them easy to recognize. Their tendency to build nests on the protected ledges of barns, houses, and bridges explained why they liked my garage's extended overhangs.

The following spring a third nest appeared almost overnight on the front of our garage. If you guessed the occupants to be phoebes, reward yourself with a scoop of birdseed. For the first time we witnessed the multiplication of our feathery houseguests, and the process produced a mess. Envision a walkway littered with cotton balls—semi-liquid white blobs to be precise—and you understand our problem. After the hatchlings grew and left the nest, Mom and Pop Phoebe decided to have a second brood, and we endured another blitz of cotton ball bombing runs. To deter the couple's return, at the end of the summer we removed the nest and scrubbed away the bombing debris, thinking they would find another nesting site next year.

Wrong.

In the fourth year, like a military special operations team on a covert mission under the cover of night, the phoebes constructed a new nest in the same spot. Once again I retrieved my bird book and educated myself on eastern phoebes. Turns out our house and their nesting habits match perfectly. They prefer the edge of woodlands, an abundant food supply, a location no higher than fifteen feet above ground, and a convenient water source for constructing their mud and grass nests. The paragraph describing their propensity to use the same nest year after year concerned me the most. No doubt a family of phoebes designated my garage as a highly desirable neighborhood. After another long summer of watching where we stepped near the garage doors, we removed the nest and planned preventive measures for the future.

On the recommendation of bird experts, we installed stainless steel strips of bird repelling spikes along the garage's front exterior rafter. The phoebes could use the back rafter all they wanted, but we wouldn't tolerate their mess on the front where we walked daily. According to the product's advertising, the toothpick-sized spikes wouldn't harm the birds but would discourage them from perching or building nests. Yippee! We looked forward to a clean sidewalk next spring.

Wrong again.

We were now in year five. One day in late March, I stared out the window over my kitchen sink and spotted a bowl-shaped mud and moss bird nest on the front porch ledge. Surprise, our garage-loving phoebes decided to move closer to us. My bird book stated that the female primarily constructed the nest, taking between five and fourteen days to complete it.

Baloney.

This particular female slapped it up overnight and added the final touches while I gawked at her architectural wonder. How embarrassing. A bird brain outmaneuvered two adults who thought they possessed above-average intelligence. To make matters worse, she and her singing partner taunted us by lounging on the porch's stone pillars and acting like they owned the place. As payback for the garage rafter bird spikes, they perched on our porch furniture and left behind multiple white calling cards. The ultimate insult occurred when they produced five new fuzzy offspring.

Weeks later when the youngsters learned to fly, our porch resembled an airport runway attacked by an Air Force squadron shooting paintball guns. In case you're wondering, the removal of dried white paint requires considerable scrubbing. As a counteroffensive measure for next March, I ordered more boxes of stainless steel bird spikes. We removed the nest in September and installed the strips along the porch eaves. Four can play this chess game, Momma Phoebe. I dared her to find another suitable building spot on my porch.

She did.

Year six. The winged genius performed something close to a construction miracle. To comprehend her achievement, think of the world's tallest building, highest dam, or longest bridge squeezed into a space half its size. A few phoebe nest facts provide additional context. The outside diameter measures about five inches across when completed, and the inside diameter is two and a half inches with a two-inch depth. Momma Phoebe must have taken an engineering class during the winter because she tailored her new nest to fit into a ninety-degree corner on the one-inch ledge of the breezeway porch connecting our house to the garage. How the little smarty feathers managed to build any nest on the tiny ledge is beyond me. As additional evidence of her high IQ and clever undercover skills, we never saw her in the area or discovered the new construction site until she completed the nest. My first clue appeared as mud splatters on the steps. With no recent rain, I couldn't figure out the mud source—until I heard the familiar "phoebe" call and looked up. Momma Phoebe stood on her mini-nest like a queen on a castle balcony, waving to her subjects standing below. Her brownish-gray tail wagged up and down at me as if to say, "Checkmate, you silly human."

Talk about embarrassment. Once again, a bird brain outsmarted me, and this time she boasted about it to my face. When I broke the news to my husband, he thought I was kidding. No way a small bird found a means to plaster a wad of mud in that petite space. The old saying "Seeing is believing" comes to mind because he didn't believe me until he saw the evidence. The only positive and publishable thought crossing my mind focused on the hope that a smaller nest guaranteed fewer future bombers.

After six years of defeat, I experienced no delight in watching two new ace bombers land multiple strikes on my breezeway. With acres of woods to roam and fertilize, the juvenile twosome chose my concrete walkway as their favorite target. What an honor. As a farewell gift before they flew off to begin their new lives, the dynamic duo threw a phoebe party on the two outdoor lights beside my front door. The lantern-shaped sconces transformed into snowcapped mountains overnight. Hint—no snow falls in the south during May, at least where I live. To say I griped while scrubbing my porch, the lights, and my walkway is an understatement. Sure, I wanted them clean, but I dislike housework, inside and outside, especially when I didn't make the mess. All I thought about the entire day was payback. What other safe and effective bird nest preventatives were available? Forget the advice of bird experts lacking the brains and products to deter Mrs. Phoebe. I ditched their recommendations and resorted to natural defenses, vowing to suffer defeat no more.

Year seven. Since Mrs. Phoebe preferred the south side of structures, I concentrated my efforts on the breezeway's southern ledges. By early March, every inch of potential nesting space contained a sharp-edged rock small enough to fit on the narrow interior edge. No way Wonder Bird built a nest on a rocky, sharp, and uneven surface. No way, I said to myself each morning as I surveyed the area for covert activity. No way, I told my husband every evening when I completed my second walk of the perimeter. No way, I repeated to my reflection in the bathroom mirror while brushing my teeth before bed.

Guess what?

By Callie Smith Grant's deadline to submit this story, I'm relieved to report no signs of a phoebe nest attached to any structure on my property. Do I feel guilty for depriving a family of the use of my house? No way. Acres of woods surround me, and hundreds of trees exist for use as a nesting spot. From my spotless porch I see several knotholes in the pine trees down the south ridge perfectly suitable for you-know-who.

Have I reclaimed my house for good? If yes, I'm overjoyed at the absence of bombing debris. I also wish all phoebes living near my home a long and healthy life, but only if they nest someplace away from my house. If I later discover I've been outsmarted another year, I promise to treat the visiting victors with respect and plot against them in the future.

Regardless of the outcome, I tip my hat in admiration to the opposing team's creativity and tenacity in our protracted competition of wits. While I wear a hat outside to shield my face from the sun, in recent years I found it handy in protecting my entire head from my opponents' aerial bombardments. To their brainy credit and despite their messy deposits, eastern phoebes represent the world's avian population well. They know what they need to do each season of their lives, commit their little but mighty bird brains to accomplishing the tasks, persevere during trying circumstances, improvise when necessary, and don't quit until completing their mission. If every human being demonstrated the same fine qualities, the world would be a much better place to live.

thirty-four

A Hen Named Henrietta

CATHERINE ULRICH BRAKEFIELD

Henrietta brought to life one of my favorite childhood stories, *The Little Red Hen*. I loved it when my mother read it to me, and later in life, I read this story to my children. The Little Red Hen's struggles, and the ultimate victory she achieved, are lessons even humans can relate to. So it was with Henrietta's story.

What I learned from the Little Red Hen was all I knew about chickens. That was all about to change.

One Easter my husband, Edward, and I decided to give our grandchildren little chicks to cuddle. Edward and I decided to purchase a half dozen chicks, and when the children lost interest, we would keep them at our place.

Tractor Supply, and many local hardware stores that never had a large supply of chicks before, began to increase the stock of baby chicks because of the public's growing demands. You name the color, they had them. You name a duckling, they had them. Including the feeders, chicken warmers, waterers, everything you needed to make your little chicks happy.

The best part of this experience was speaking to the people who hovered around the horse-watering troughs now turned into nests for poultry. These people had a wealth of information and shared their tried-and-true advice with us greenhorns.

Edward and I learned that chickens were totally defenseless against every predator that roamed, day or night. Hawks would seek a tasty treat and snatch them up with their clawed feet. Owls did the same in the night. We had to make a special chicken coop and dug down a foot to place chicken wire so predators could not dig beneath the coop to get to them. When the sun took its leave, so did the chickens, and they would go find their favorite roosting spot on their perch. Without the chicken wire, skunks and raccoons could crawl up and grab them without a struggle.

I looked into that trough at Tractor Supply at those tiny yellow chicks and didn't bat an eye when we bought a new stainless steel watering trough, filled it with shavings, and placed our new chicks inside. Complete with a waterer, a feeder, and a heating lamp to keep them warm.

After all, what else could I do? They needed mothering until they could fend for themselves. And every spring after that, when we would purchase more chicks, we learned a bit more about the wonders of God's creatures.

But nothing in those years of raising chicks prepared us for Henrietta.

My husband purchased Henrietta from an Amish farm. She was a little under a year old, thin and shy. Her previous owners sold her to us primarily because she was too nervous to lay eggs. It was easy to see why.

We noted sadly her lackluster brownish-tan feathers next to our gray and black Plymouth Rocks and Rhode Island Reds.

I always wondered how the term "pecking order" became a common phrase for horse herds, cattle—and people. Watching each hen take their turn pecking at Henrietta, I figured the term had to have been coined by a person watching bossy hens.

If schoolchildren could watch barnyard chickens in action, they might not be so inclined to pick on kids on the playground. Edward and I watched in agony, knowing there was nothing we could do—because Henrietta refused to stand up for herself.

The only one that didn't peck her or treat her badly was our Rhode Island Red rooster named Red. He was a gentleman as roosters go. He'd been picked on by his brother, so maybe that's why he took an immediate liking to Henrietta. We put them together, hoping Red might defend her against the other hens. It seemed to work; the hens stopped picking on her when we put her back in the chicken coop.

It wasn't long before we noticed Henrietta sitting on her nest and refusing to get up. We never had a hen lay on her eggs before, but we were curious to see what would happen. It was around the Fourth of July when Henrietta finally rose from her nest. There were two little chicks amidst the seven eggs Henrietta had sat on. That was all. Now what?

"Poor Henrietta," I said. "All that work, and all she got was two chicks out of it."

We didn't know what to do with the other eggs. Edward waited for a few more days and then took the eggs out. We discovered that one chick had refused to hatch, and the rest of the eggs were rotten. We felt terrible and wondered if we'd been more patient, would the other chick have hatched?

Around that time, the 4-H Fair in Davisburg was in full swing, and we decided to go with some friends. It so happened that dozens of chicks had hatched that day in the birthing barn. Edward began talking to one of the 4-H leaders.

"They're willing to sell us five chicks that hatched a day ago," Edward said. "This way, we'll be replacing Henrietta's eggs that didn't hatch."

"But would Henrietta accept these chicks?" I asked.

We asked the director in charge.

She shrugged her shoulders. "I haven't a clue."

No one could give us an answer.

The question really came down to, Would Henrietta, who had been bullied, in turn bully her adopted chicks? There was a fifty-fifty chance this could happen.

"It's a fact that if a cow births two calves, she could disown one of them," I said. "We're asking a lot from a hen."

Edward was more practical minded. "They are just chicks, not babies. And they can survive on their own—they just need to be kept warm."

"I know." But I could not get it out of my mind. "How sad, if Henrietta doesn't take these little chicks, and they remain orphans, knowing no mommy."

We and a friend who had come along with us picked out five chicks and paid for them. The Michigan State University 4-H leader boxed the chicks, and off we went with the newly hatched day-old birds. Either to be basking under a heat lamp or in the loving embrace of Henrietta, their new mom.

This would prove an experience for us all.

That same day, we herded our flock of chickens and rooster to the outside coop and placed the little chicks in the inside coop. Our one hope was that it was a warm July afternoon and maybe the chicks could survive for a day not basking in the incubator.

Henrietta approached the new chicks. We held our breaths. This was a critical time. She clucked low, then turned and began eating. That was it? What did this mean?

"Maybe we should give her some time alone with them," Edward said.

I nodded, afraid to utter a word for fear he'd notice my disappointment. Reluctantly we left.

Walking toward the house, I imagined the outcome: returning to see all five chicks dead from Henrietta's stab wounds. All she knew was being bullied. Henrietta's mother hadn't protected her, so why should Henrietta protect some orphaned chicks?

After we had our dinner, we walked to the barn to bring our horses in and tend to the chickens.

Nothing had changed from early afternoon. Henrietta was scratching around and eating and ignoring the new chicks in the coop.

"Maybe this is good," I said. "It's warm enough for them in the coop, don't you think?"

"Now, but what about tonight?" Edward replied.

Later, nestled in our chairs with a bowl of popcorn between us, I tried to concentrate on the movie we were watching. It was around 10 p.m.

"Should we go and check on the chicks?" I asked. "It's probably too cold for them tonight without being under a heat lamp."

"Natural-born chicks don't have heat lamps. How do they stay warm?"

Edward asked a good question. The chickens always picked a spot on the ladder he placed in the hen coop to roost on for the night. Where would the chicks go? They couldn't fly up there.

"I'll go out and check on them," Edward said.

I got the heat lamp we use for our new chicks ready, just in case, and changed for bed. By now it was around eleven o'clock, and I was tired from a very busy and trying day at the 4-H fairgrounds.

Edward appeared inside the bedroom door, all smiles. He had a flashlight in his hands. "Come on, I want you to see this."

Putting on my bathrobe, I followed him.

There on their roost sat Henrietta, and beneath her wings were the wee heads of her own two chicks and the five orphaned ones. That scene brought tears to my eyes. How the chicks got up there and situated beneath her wings is one of those wonderful miracles of nature. But I have stopped trying to outthink God—his ways are not our ways.

We'll never forget Henrietta, nor those chicks hatched in an incubator—who knew by instinct what to do when their adoptive mom covered them beneath her loving wings!

Henrietta found the courage she had lacked. No one was going to bully her little chicks! And so, the chickens abandoned their game of bullying and watched in humble adoration as Henrietta and her happy chicks strutted around the barnyard.

Henrietta brought one of my favorite stories, *The Little Red Hen*, to life. Since then, my daughter and son have purchased chickens, but not a single one ever came close to being another Henrietta. Just like the Little Red Hen of my favorite barnyard story, the hen named Henrietta made it into a story all her own.

thirty-five

Talking to the Birds

MARCI KLADNIK

"How would you like to come with me this afternoon to help call out a pygmy owl?" my mother asked. "They're rare, and one has just been spotted in town."

I have always been blessed with what is called a "good ear." Not only has music been a big part of my life but I also have an ability to mimic some sounds in nature. Particularly birds.

My mother was very impressed with my talent, as she was an avid birder. The attempt to call out the pygmy owl that afternoon was a bust, but had I had time to study the bird and listen to its song, the outcome might have been different.

I was a very shy child and so spent a lot of time communing with nature. I'd spend hours on my belly, watching bugs in the dirt or blue-belly lizards sunning themselves on the warm rocks. Sometimes my bike took me to the harbor, where I watched the crabs scuttling on the anemone-covered rocks as the Pacific Ocean waves splashed over them. On other days, I'd walk through groves of scrub oaks with their dry leaves crunching beneath my feet.

Everywhere I went there were birds.

There were the trips to the bird refuge to feed the ducks when I was very little. My parents were good at introducing us children to the wonders of nature. My brother, sister, and I took these lessons to heart as we grew older, but my budding talent led me to a higher level.

Out of habit, I studied the sounds of birds and animals as I interacted with them or watched from afar. Gradually their calls imprinted on my brain without me realizing it, and soon I was able to "talk" back to them.

The seagulls were fun to feed bits of sandwich to during lunchtime at school. A screaming flock of them would swoop down, and I'd toss a crust in the air, watching as it was expertly snatched and carried away by the closest and fastest bird. I didn't call back to them, however, because I was a young teenager in middle school and I was already considered a bit odd.

But it was the doves that touched my heart and opened up my gift to a new level. I have fond memories of standing in our California backyard, calling mourning doves to me. It never failed that one would answer and fly down to check out the new bird, only to be disappointed to find a human instead of another dove.

It wasn't just mourning doves that I was able to imitate. I could bark like the sea lions and speak cat.

As an adult I spent hundreds of hours trapping and caring for feral cats and their kittens, and as a result I learned some of their language. I became so good at it that I was able to coax kittens out of hiding by mimicking a mother calling her kittens to her.

There is something magical in communicating with another living species, even if I don't know what I'm saying most of the time. Even now in my seventies, I still try to communicate with the animals I pet sit for. I have been told on many occasions that some of my charges are very shy and don't take to strangers well, but they respond to me. Just imagine how wonderful it would be to be like the character Dr. Doolittle and really talk with them.

Learning bird sounds, or any other language, takes time and patience. I didn't intend to learn the mourning dove call, it just happened one day when I was listening to them. When I realized that I could call back and they would answer, I was thrilled. From then on, every time I would hear them calling, I'd join in the conversation just for fun.

When I moved to a different part of California, the doves that came to my backyard were ring-necked doves singing a different song. Their calls were very similar to the mourning dove, so it was easy for me to learn the new dialect.

I also learned to call the big owls that roosted on the rooftops of the houses and in the tops of the tall trees near my new home. They hunted in the agricultural fields at night and occasionally were known to snatch a cat or two in town.

I remember one night when I was lounging on the couch with a sleeping cat on my lap. Suddenly the hooting of a large owl came down the chimney into the room. On impulse I called back, freaking the cat out so much that he left claw marks on my leg as he jumped from my lap and ran off to hide. Apparently I had nailed that owl hoot.

Recently I moved to Wisconsin, so now I have a whole new set of birds and animals to study. I'm in the process of turning my yard into a wildlife park, forgoing the huge expanse of lawn for trees, shrubs, flowers, and an all-important pond that will support a variety of critters, especially birds and butterflies.

I'm happy to say that I have already mastered some of the calls of the beautiful cardinals that come to my deck to feed and nest in the nearby trees. Time will tell if I will be able to call one to me, as they are rather shy birds. But for now, it's just really fun to send out that call and hear a reply.

thirty-six

Free

JOAN SOGGIE

"You could sometimes let Paulette out of her cage to fly around
the house, okay? But please, be sure to put her back in her cage
before you go out!"

My husband was going to be home alone with the pets for a
whole week while our kids and I embarked on some summer
adventures. My head was full of doubts and concerns. With
harvesttime fast approaching, I worried that he might need my
help. And I was concerned about Andrea's budgie.

The kids and I agreed: That budgie was not doing well. If
ever a bird seemed depressed, it was Paulette. Given to Andrea
for her eleventh birthday and showered with love and attention,
Paulette perked up only when an occasional flock of sparrows
swooped into view outside the window by her perch.

Now she sat hunched, feathers fluffed, in the corner of her
clean, comfortable cage, staring dolefully out the living room

window. It was going to be a long week for that little bird, I thought.

But for the rest of us, the week sped by. Andrea and her school friend found fun and adventure at camp with a batch of energetic preteens. Teenagers Neil and Lori worked on their football and volleyball skills and made new friends at the university coed sports camp. College student Kim and I headed north to join a group of adults and teens on a wilderness canoe camping trip.

It was a week of discovery for each of us. I cannot presume to know exactly what my children learned, but I discovered the heart-pounding exhilaration of sweeping into sudden rapids, our canoe buffeted and drenched as my intrepid daughter laughed and shouted, "Paddle! Paddle harder!"

Andrea told us about her last day of camp, when for some reason the boys were each required to invite a girl to accompany him to the windup banquet. Not one but two boys had invited her.

"How did you choose?"

"Well, one of them cried . . ."

Lori and Neil talked about the coaches, the games, and the other kids they had met. There was a new confidence in their voices. It had been a good week for them too.

We all felt bigger, stronger, changed. And when we got home, we saw changes there too. Harvest was late, and Dennis had decided to use the fine weather, a government home-renovation grant, and the absence of distractions to start building an addition on the house. Footings were poured, the cement patio was gone—and Paulette was gone too.

"I guess I forgot about her—just opened the screen door for a sec and she flew out."

I wouldn't have admitted it, but I was secretly relieved. It would be an easier loss for Andrea to accept than finding her budgie lying beak open and toes curled in the bottom of the cage.

The surprise came a few days later. Andrea was with me in the car as we returned from some errand. A flock of sparrows fluttered across the road in front of us. I was reminded of how Paulette used to hop around her cage and chirp at the sparrows outside her window as my eyes followed their flight. Suddenly I slammed on the brakes and whooped.

"Look, Andrea! Do you see that?"

There was Paulette, a pale-yellow budgie flying with the quick brown sparrows. She mimicked their flight, swooping and turning and landing in the grass. Paulette had found her flock.

After that we saw her almost every day. Sometimes she would let Andrea approach within a few feet before flying away. Once or twice she left her flock briefly to swoop over us, as though she were showing off her rapidly improving flying skills. But it was abundantly clear that she had no intention of returning to the safety of her cage. The wisdom of this wild bunch of sparrows was her safety now.

Sometimes after a rainstorm I would see her splashing in an almost freezing puddle, joining the sparrows in their puddle bath. And I shook my head, recalling how, even though I used to warm the water to body temperature in a shallow dish for her, she had shivered and sulked over the indignity of being wet. Now, nothing dampened her enthusiasm.

August passed. September came. The children all went back to school. Harvest was in full swing. Coffee shop gossip mulled over the mystery of the albino sparrow, until our local newspaper correspondent explained in her column that it was Andrea's escaped budgie. Then, it seemed, everyone watched for her. Neighbors from miles around would call to tell us they had seen Paulette, at their farm or across the street or by the grain elevators. The nights grew cold, and the first snow fell. Still she flew with her flock of sparrows.

The last reported sighting came in mid-November.

We will never know what finally took that brave little life, but, thirty-five years later, I still think of her every once in a while. It seems to me that she epitomizes something we all long for but are often afraid to grasp.

Freedom.

It's scary to be free. The week that Paulette flew away, we each had our own taste of freedom, and we each had been, to some degree, terrified. Dennis must have been at least a little nervous about my reaction to the back wall of the house being torn off, but he boldly started his renovation project anyway. As exhilarating as it was to shoot the rapids with my intrepid daughter, my heart also pounded with fear at the thought of capsizing and losing my glasses. Kim came on the canoe trip exhausted from six weeks of French immersion that she said was the hardest thing she had ever done in all her nineteen years and continued to sleep-talk in French every night of our camping trip. Lori and Neil faced the unknown at the sports camp, jumping in with strangers from bigger and better schools, risking rejection . . . almost the scariest thing any teenager can do. Andrea had her first week away from home by herself and followed compassion into an uncomfortable situation. Each of us grew a little because we dared to choose freedom over safety.

Our kids flew from our nest long ago. They have assumed the burdens of adulthood, taken charge of their own lives, lived with the consequences of their choices. Maybe they sometimes feel caged by the responsibilities of careers and parenthood, but they know that responsibility is just the flip side of the freedom coin. And now it is their kids, our grandchildren, who are experiencing their own hard, exhilarating freedom lessons.

And still, every time I think I cannot do something, that I am too old or too weak or too foolish, I think of that silly bird. If she could do it, then what am I waiting for?

thirty-seven

Mom and Midge

CLAUDIA WOLFE ST. CLAIR

While going through craft supplies this morning, I found a carefully sealed sandwich bag of feathers. They had been packed away by my mother years ago. Whenever her bird, Midge, lost a feather, Mom saved it. Here they were now, calling up memories of Mom and Midge.

Early in my mother's widowhood, she decided she wanted a cockatiel to keep her company. A friend recommended a source for hand-raised hatchlings. It wasn't long before she was the proud owner of a young, gray cockatiel with a yellow crown.

At first, she didn't have a name in mind. Mom would just coo at her in soft tones, "You're my bird," giving her a kiss on the beak.

We talked about the bird at length, Mom in Ohio, me in Virginia. Her favorite book series published in the forties had a character with a bird she took everywhere. Its name was Midge.

I reminded Mom about the story. It was like a light bulb lit up. Midge was the perfect name for her new companion.

Midge had everything a bird could want, a spacious cage with all the fancy accoutrements necessary to keep her healthy and entertained. She also had a doting human who allowed her total freedom.

During the day Midge was hardly in the cage at all. She walked along the windowsills on the lake side of the house. She flew to the top of mirrors and pictures on the walls. She especially enjoyed the vanity mirror in the bathroom.

At night she was in her cage, covered and in the bedroom with Mom. They were together 24/7 with an open-door policy. Not even the bathroom was off limits.

Midge's favorite place to perch was anywhere near or on Mom. The back or arms of Mom's chair were fair game. Mom's shoulder was better. Her knees would do in a pinch. Best of all was on Mom's head, where she could tug Mom's hair for fun.

Midge walked all over the dining room table at mealtimes. There were no boundaries. If the food looked interesting, Midge was free to taste Mom's meal. After Midge jumped into Mom's salad one night, a line had to be drawn. The solution was a separate little salad for Midge. Problem solved. Thus began the training of my mother by her bird companion.

Because Mom was an intrepid traveler, Midge also required a travel case to carry birdseed, cuttlebones, bones, bells, and assorted bits and bobs for their trips east to be with us in Virginia. They were frequent and lengthy visitors.

There was only one rule at my house. Midge must stay in her cage. Of course, Mom broke that rule as soon as I left for work. They were like two naughty children. Putting something over on me was the greatest game of all.

For some years Midge's gender was not known. One Christmas that was clarified definitively.

Midge started behaving aggressively toward anyone sitting near the cage. Hissing, rushing toward the offender with wings flapping and debris from the cage flying out in all directions. It was a mess. The only way to calm the frantic bird was to cover the cage. This behavior went on for days.

One evening I was the one sitting beside the birdcage. Midge hopped back up on one of the perches. There in the corner on the floor of the cage was an egg.

"Mom? Midge is a female. Look!"

She had been agitated for days in her first labor and defending her egg all this time. Who knew? The evening took a celebratory turn.

We learned a lot about bird behavior as a result. When a bird bonds with its human, it considers itself mated. Once a female reaches maturity, she can lay unfertilized eggs. Midge began laying eggs prolifically from then on.

Upon their return to Ohio, Midge was back to her life of unbounded freedom. She laid eggs wherever it suited. Mom found them all over the house and saved them in a crystal bowl, where they dried out. She kept them for years.

When Midge molted, Mom saved the long feathers. Those are the ones I found this morning.

There is a favorite story about one of the eggs that has become legendary in our family lore.

Mom was inclined to doze off in her chair most afternoons. Remember, Midge's favorite out-of-cage perch was my mother. Upon waking, Mom found a freshly laid egg sitting in the middle of her chest! The ultimate gift of love Midge could give.

This morning, finding the feathers feels like a gift of love too. I live in the house by the lake now, like Mom, in my widowhood. I enjoy the birds I can see from my windows. The echoes indoors of all who have gone before me is enough. Once in a while I find a feather on the rug and know for certain they are all near.

thirty-eight

Taught to Soar

SUSAN M. WATKINS

Driving home from work one evening after a heavyhearted day, I stopped in a small pet shop to see about a possible pet for my young daughter. The bell above the door alerted the shopkeeper that he had a potential sale before closing, and he immediately ingratiated himself to me.

As he showed me an array of possibilities, I paused at the tumbling puppies but had to move on to something much smaller. "Do you have a home or apartment?" he queried. Having recently moved, I answered, "A small condo, so I was thinking about a bird." This unfolded road map took us past fish tanks and straight to the large cage at the back of the store filled with chirping and squawking parakeets. Having been raised with them, I had an idea of what to look for but wasn't prepared for so many choices.

The cage contained a rainbow of colorful birds flapping about to claim perch space. But then I spotted the only white beauty

Consider the Birds

among the others. I'd never seen a bird like him before and asked his price. "Well, that one is a fancy parakeet so he's the most expensive one in there," said the owner. Yet this parakeet caught my eye. Not just because of his beauty but because I sensed there was something special about him. Watching him actively hop from perch to perch and never engage in territory wars underscored he was exactly what my heartbroken daughter needed.

After selecting his new cage with all the necessary accessories, toys, and food, I found that the purchases totaled more than I could comfortably spend. The older man intuitively asked why my little girl needed a pet. I hesitated but shared her heartbreak.

Our life had recently been upended, and in addition to my full-time job and downsizing to a smaller apartment, she'd begun attending school. The school had just had a father-daughter dance, which my little one was unable to attend, and her classmates were making fun of her for only having a mother. I wanted to get her something she could care for and call her own, and a bird was all that would fit in our new home.

Dabbing his tears, the shopkeeper unexpectedly recalculated my total, put my fancy bird in a box, then carried my purchases to my car. I wiped my tears, hugged and thanked him, then drove away with my surprise scratching about beside me and peeking through the air holes of his temporary home. While driving, I carefully explained his new mission.

It seemed like an ordinary day at our new address when I parked in the driveway that evening. My little girl heard me pull up and ran to her bedroom window that overlooked my car. We excitedly waved at one another before she disappeared from view. She'd be kissing and hugging me within moments, so I quickly hid her bird. Seeing the birdcage confused her, and a flood of questions ensued.

"Mommy, what do you need that thing for?" she asked.

"Oh, it's for something very special," I answered matter-of-factly.

Her curiosity piqued, forcing her to investigate further. "Is it for us or someone else?" she questioned while hopping sideways toward the front door.

"You'll see in just a moment," I stated while suppressing my happy secret.

Her loud excitement reached the house before she did and summoned her grandmother and playful partner in crime who'd come to live with us. Mom took one surprised look at the cage and knew exactly what I was hiding. Sitting my kindergartener down, I explained I needed her to be extra quiet as I'd brought her something very special, and we couldn't frighten it.

Her eyes widened like saucers as she leaned in. Having just readied the cage for occupancy, I brought out the bird box and told her I had to put its contents directly into the cage for now. As she excitedly covered her mouth with her hands, I gently put the small bird with a huge assignment into its home within a home. My daughter squealed before screaming with delight into a nearby pillow. Otherwise, her shout would have been heard in a one-mile radius.

With Mom smiling and knowingly nodding her head, my daughter asked in hushed anticipation, "Is it ours? Is this birdie ours?"

"No, Sweet Pea," I said, "he isn't ours." Her shoulders dropped before I could finish, and I quickly clarified, "He's all yours! This is your bird."

Complete pandemonium ensued as my daughter ran between her grandmother and me, hugging and thanking us. She even hugged the birdcage. I told her she could name him whatever she wished, and after seriously evaluating him for a few moments, she proudly announced, "His name is Snowflake because he looks like snow!" It was the perfect name, for he was white with touches of frosty blue and a tail longer than typically seen on a juvenile parakeet. She very gently stroked his crown with her finger, which caused him to close his eyes rather than bite in fear.

With that, I knew the Lord had led me to the perfect bird, and their journey began.

Armed with feathery ammunition, she returned to school gushing about her white bird. The school dance was quickly forgotten as her classmates listened in awe as she told them about Snowflake. She couldn't wait to tell us about her day and how everyone was so happy for her. Barely an ounce of feathers with a tweet righted her world and challenged her to bravely soar. Snowflake became a salve for her heart.

The little budgie slept in my child's bedroom every night from then on. At first I was concerned he'd keep her awake, but instead his singing lulled her to sleep. They became inseparable.

I quickly went to task training this young parakeet, as Mom had trained all of ours in my childhood. He was still so young that his hidden blue feathers under his wings were barely visible. But the cere at the top of his beak was bright blue.

As Snowflake grew, his list of tricks followed close behind. He became free range in the sense he spent his waking hours outside his cage if so desired. We left the door open for him to come and go as he pleased. He would hop in to eat and drink, then come back out to scan his territory from above. We would find him perched on curtain or shower rods, picture frames, cabinet tops, light fixtures, and even sitting on the outside of his cage. He also loved all the furniture, every possible table, and enjoyed hopping across my daughter's bed as I read to her at night. Once he successfully learned to come when called and perch on someone's extended finger, he had the run of the house. It was a delight to see he fully trusted all of us.

He'd also sing for his supper, which were special bird treats, lettuce, or orange slices. Mom was always able to whistle exactly like a bird and could call down twenty or more wild birds out of the trees. I have many vivid memories of this as a child, and our backyard regulars waited for her to exit the house, then lined up like clothespins along the clothesline to join her aria. Snowflake especially enjoyed accompanying her in song, looking at her in admiration, either on her shoulder or from another room.

The day arrived for his first out-of-the-cage bath time. He'd been taking baths in his cage with the bathtub hung over the open door, but his tail feathers were so long that he couldn't turn around anymore to reach all his necessary spots. I filled a pie plate with warm water and transferred him from cage to rim on my finger. He examined it thoroughly, cocking his head back and forth and dancing left to right along the rim—then dove in and splashed around in circles in sheer delight, emptying the pan of its water. My daughter gleefully giggled, which encouraged her feathered pet to do more antics for her. They'd each tilt their heads side-to-side at one another, and sometimes Snowflake was so delighted with her that he'd take to flight and circle the house before returning to her shoulder. He also loved dancing on top of a large mirror I'd lay on the table while mesmerized by his reflection. His dance routine elicited laughter from my child, which only encouraged Snowflake to dance and twirl faster while whistling.

As months passed, this unusual bird began to cuddle against my daughter's neck. He'd land on her shoulder and sidestep across until reaching her neck. Once tucked into his spot, he'd fluff out his feathers then cuddle up close and lean against her, sitting there for hours.

I watched as Snowflake became self-taught. He decided to perch on top of our heads. Wings fully spread and angled for drag to slow him, he'd carefully drop on the tops of our heads like a 747 airplane on final approach. Then he would contentedly stay there like it was his nest. This was my daughter's most favorite trick, and once he was there, he would preen nearly the entire time. After grooming himself, he'd turn his attention to the rest of his "flock" and begin preening us. Delicately grasping a clump of hair in his beak, he'd twist it around until satisfied before moving onto the next group. That goofy bird styled all of our hair but spent the majority of his time on the smallest member of his flock. He spent hours in the "nest" of her hair, repositioning her bows. He left only long enough to eat or drink before returning. Eventually he was such a fixture in her hair, posing as an Easter bonnet, that you'd no longer notice him or find it unusual. Like salt is to pepper, so Snowflake was to my daughter.

He also enjoyed spending time with me. I'd be busy doing chores or cooking, and suddenly there he was, whistling on my shoulder or head. Active movements rarely bothered him, and he'd hold on tighter rather than fly off.

He'd even go for rides in the car and sat next to my girl in his cage while they shared secrets.

Our snowy parakeet was also a fixture at the breakfast table. Breakfast was his favorite meal, as it was the only time he'd share our table food. Tap dancing across the hard surface, he'd enjoy the crumbs from our toast. With skillful accuracy he'd grasp the small bits then move on to the next benefactor. It was breakfast and a show.

There was never a question as to why God created this specific bird. Snowflake had purpose beyond sitting in a cage and squawking, and there was a reason I was drawn to him years ago in that pet store. Snowflake had an innate sensitivity to my daughter's emotions and lovingly responded to her with his entire one and a half ounces of joyfulness. He readily healed her broken heart but also taught her courage, resilience, adaptability, and to always soar above the fray.

Years passed, addresses changed, but one thing was solid: This sweet budgie was the perfect pet for our family. Coming home after a challenging day and rush-hour traffic, I'd be greeted by a bird who could outmaneuver my precious girl's speed. Plopping on my head, he'd struggle to stay there as I bent down to hug and kiss my Sweet Pea. At times I wondered if that silly bird had spent too much time watching the puppies in that kind owner's pet shop, because at times he acted like a dog.

I'd often stop by that pet shop to pick up supplies and shock the shopkeeper with stories of our bird's behavior. Even he agreed how unusual it was. He knew he'd been a direct part of my daughter's happiness by selling his fancy bird at a price I could afford and was thrilled to eventually meet her.

There were even additions to Snowflake's flock. As my daughter grew and had greater responsibilities, I suggested we get Snowflake a companion. Delighted with this idea, we both went to our favorite pet shop and found another fancy parakeet. She was white and aqua and so pretty that my daughter named her Beauty. The ever-sociable Snowflake was overjoyed and heartily welcomed her to his home. We tried to teach Beauty the same tricks Snowflake knew, but she was content to stay inside the cage. Snowflake still flew around like always and nested in our hair, but not as much since Beauty was afraid to join him and he liked to keep her company. Eventually, we added another budgie from the same store. This time my growing daughter found a very timid blue and white bird huddled in the corner of the cage, trying to stay away from the other birds. The store owner confessed that he was having trouble selling him because he had only one eye and was so timid. That was all it took for my compassionate daughter, who pleaded with me to purchase him. I looked at the owner who'd been so kind to my child those many years ago and told him to box up that little budgie. My daughter named him Timidthy. All three were happy singers in their new large cage, but it was later determined that three's a crowd, so another visit to the pet shop was in order. We chose a female aptly named Rainbow, due to her green and yellow feathers and brilliant pink beak. She rounded out our budgerigar menagerie.

Eventually Snowflake's earthly journey reached its end. It was hard to say goodbye to a family pet who had been such a loving part of our lives. He got my daughter through some very difficult years as they connected on a level I never thought was possible. He went above and beyond the purpose for his life and blessed my family in remarkable and surprising ways. My daughter had extra tenacity because of him.

Snowflake will always have a piece of my heart, but this is nothing compared to what he shared with my daughter, who is now an adult with children of her own. She still asks, "Mom, remember Snowflake?" And the memories pour out as we talk about him decades later and look at the adorable photos of him dancing on his mirror, bathing in his pie plate, or sitting atop her head.

Never underestimate the gift God lovingly sends to fly into your hands. It may just touch a place in your heart you never knew existed.

thirty-nine

The Tiny but Mighty
Mama Bird

NICOLE M. MILLER

Today we woke to the first chick hatched in our incubator—our first ever raised in a store-bought incubator rather than the God-made incubator called a hen. As with most first experiences, there's a strange sense of unease, the unknown, and true wonder.

And during this time, I can't help but think about a special chicken we inherited, who was the first one to show us the incredible design of hatching chickens from our own flock's eggs. Her name was Showgirl, because, well, as an English game hen, she had disproportionately long legs and a compact body of smooth, dark brown feathers, and a regal head adorned with golden feathers. She was no bigger than my fist and yet had the confidence of a ten-pound rooster.

She came to our flock of twelve only a year or so into our jour-ney of raising chickens, so we clearly hadn't learned everything we were meant to learn. (Ten years later, I'm still learning.) We took her in from someone who didn't have the space anymore, along with a miniature barred rock (imagine a grey hen with black stripes and then shrink it by 40 percent) and a white Polish hen (picture a white leghorn with a tuft of upright white feathers all over her face). The three were a motley bunch, all seeming out of place, and yet they came into our flock as their own little trio and put the bigger chickens in their place.

Showgirl, more than the others, threw off the pecking order and shuffled it all about until she was near the top. Though I'd been amazed by the personalities and sheer drama that comes from one cluster of fowl, everything was tipped on its head when we added new personalities to the mix. The backyard was full of clucking, screeching, and indignant wing flapping, from dawn till dusk.

This little hen boasted the largest and most piercing cluck of any bird in relation to her overall mass—she had the most unique chirps and calls, always identifiable from across the yard.

Day to day, Showgirl led her little trio around the sea of green grass in our long, narrow backyard, and I lost track of how often I'd just watch them and laugh. She even dominated the four ducks as they waddled and quacked about nonchalantly.

With free-ranging our flock, every day became an Easter-egg hunt to find whatever new spot the girls preferred as their nest for that day. As fussy as they were about who left or entered the coop first at daylight or day's end, they also bickered over who laid their eggs in the new, random location.

And occasionally, one of the hens would turn broody and decide that those eggs would become her charge to incubate and raise.

We'd always been quick to remove the eggs and shoo the hen away to keep her as a layer instead of a broody hen that won't lay eggs.

But when we saw little Showgirl perched atop four perfectly pristine eggs—two green, two light brown—we didn't have the heart to dislodge her. She was in a small nesting box we'd put in the corner of the coop, so she was safe from the outside elements and would be locked up at night.

She seemed so determined. She'd ruffle out all of her feathers and settle over the four eggs, covering every edge with precision. If anyone came near, she'd arch her neck and chirp out deep, guttural warnings.

Why not? If we lost four eggs, that was fine, and if she was able to actually hatch out chicks, that'd be . . . well, we just didn't really expect that little bantam hen to be able to fully insulate and bring the eggs to term.

In the busyness of life, the twenty-one days to incubate the eggs flew by, and though we checked on her morning and night with the regular chores, we didn't really expect actual results.

And I'm sure you know where this is going.

Out popped three of the four chicks, the fourth one hatching a day later. Two little Ameracaunas and two golden-laced Wyandottes. Collectively, the four chicks were as big as their nest mother, and Showgirl preened and fussed over them proudly.

We tried to replicate this over the years, letting other hens sit on eggs and deferring to nature to take its course. More often than not, things didn't work out. It almost seemed that the more we pushed or tried to recreate the magic Showgirl had with her little brood, the more we failed.

There was something special about that little hen and her heart of gold.

She raised those chicks to full-grown chickens, two of which became roosters that towered over her. One of those roosters became the kindest and most polite rooster we've ever owned. She was still always the mama bird of the four, and they constantly followed her around and bowed to her authority. Picturing her, hardly an eighth of the size of each of those fully grown chickens, still gives me such joy and affirms that not everything is as it seems. And that the resilience and strength you have within can overshadow what physical appearances might otherwise dictate.

The months drew into years, and as many free-range birds do, Showgirl disappeared one day, perhaps venturing forth to another family in the neighborhood, perhaps falling prey to all that threatened such a small creature. Her chicks endured, and one of her babies is still a part of our flock nearly eight years later, and producing the eggs we're incubating right now.

The legacy of that small, mighty mama hen lives on.

So thank you, Showgirl, for showing how mighty things can come in minuscule packages. Thank you for showcasing the magic and wonder of life and renewal. Thank you for leading the pack and blazing a trail for the hens who came after.

As I fuss and preen over the fresh hatchling in our Styrofoam incubator, I can't help but think of little Showgirl and her chicks, and the way animals of all shapes and sizes leave impressions and warm feelings on your very soul.

forty

The Messenger

LONNIE HULL DuPONT

I was very close to my mother, and I was fortunate to have her until she was eighty-four. In the end, cancer took her, but she always planned to beat it. She was determined to live. Although she had confidence in where she would be in the next life, my mother really and truly did not want to leave this one, and she fought hard to stay here.

In the last six weeks of my mother's life, with the help of hospice, she stayed at my sister's house a few country miles from my own house. During this time, Mom and I spent lots of time together, talking. I wrote in my diary then: "It's a sad time but a soft time." I knew she was dying, but she never seemed to accept it herself. Once she told me, "I sleep so well at night now. Then I wake up thinking of all the things I'm going to do, and I'm ready to jump up and do them." She seemed bewildered as she looked down at her cancer-riddled body. "And every morning, I'm so surprised that I can't."

Two days before Mom died, I dreamed I was standing in a cemetery next to my car. Two young men, both wearing dark suits and dark glasses, approached me. I felt nervous about them, so I hurried into the car and hit the lock button. They watched the locks snap down. I cracked my window, and one of them said, "Will you tell us where you're going?" I refused, and I raised the window back up. Then I turned the car around and drove away. I watched them in the rearview window to see if they would follow, but they simply watched me drive away. When I woke up, I felt God had sent me a message that I should prepare, that my mother's passing would be soon.

The next day was very difficult for Mom. She had overnight lost the ability to speak clearly. She could express herself with her eyes, gestures, and head nods or shakes, but her speech was garbled. She badly wanted to talk, and it seemed she had something important to say to us. But try as she might, she could not say it.

Finally at one point, my mother gave up trying to talk and began to keen. I do not come from a culture of people who keen, and it was a frightening sound to me. When Mom eventually quieted down, she curled into a fetal position and went into a deep sleep.

Mom was still breathing when my husband Joe and I drove to our house early that evening. We were drained from this emotionally difficult day, so we didn't talk much. We simply went to our bedroom and tuned in to the television news, prepared to turn in early. Our two cats joined us on the bed.

We lived in a large old farmhouse, and our bedroom was what had once been a front parlor. It sat next to the central hallway and front door, so when I looked out the window on my side of the bed, I could see the side of the front portico of the house.

It was almost dusk. The news blared away. I was aware of the cats running over me at some point to get to the open window on my side of the bed, and I could hear a bird, but thought nothing of it. The huge yew bushes outside the windows had lots of bird life, and that brought plenty of viewing thrills to our house cats.

Joe muted the TV and said, "Listen." The cats sat at the window, their tails slapping hard on the bedside table. There was a loud, insistent chirp coming in from the screen. I saw to my surprise one red cardinal on the yew branches, looking at the window screen, chirping hard.

I grew up in the country and of course knew some birds. But my mother really was more attuned to them. She taught me to watch for the first robin of spring, which after a long Michigan winter was wonderful to see. My mother kept bird feeders and wren houses, and she fed birds in the snow when she still wintered in Michigan. She often told me that she hated to see a bird in a cage. "They should be outdoors and flying, not caged up," she would say.

So I knew a little about birds, and while I didn't recognize the chirp of this bird, I certainly could recognize the scarlet brilliance of a male cardinal. He was so close and so loud that the cats were simply beside themselves.

Neither Joe nor I had any idea why this bird sat vocalizing fearlessly into our open window as dusk approached. He hopped from yew branch to the portico and back again, over and over, his chirping loud and insistent. One of the cats made her signature "kill" noise—a fast clicking of her back teeth—but even that didn't unnerve the cardinal. Our talking didn't, either.

"Do you think his mate is hurt or something?" I asked.

"Let's see," Joe said. We stepped outside, and the cardinal moved to the top of the portico. He did not fly away, and he did not stop chirping. We investigated the porch and surrounding grass, even under the yews, but we saw no reason for this cardinal to be so agitated. So we went indoors.

The bird moved back to the yews and window, and he continued chirping. He chirped so loud that when a friend called on the phone, I finally shut the window so I could hear her better. He chirped outside the closed window for a while longer and eventually flew away. As I fell asleep that night, it occurred to me that, like the men in the dream, perhaps the cardinal might be some kind of messenger, but I fell asleep while trying to figure it out.

At 5:00 a.m., my sister called to say we'd better come. Mom passed away a few minutes before we arrived. But seeing her body at rest made us all realize how free from pain and frustration she was now. My family and I sat next to Mom's bed for a time. Her room had an east window, and as the sun was rising, my brother-in-law remarked, "Look—a cardinal." Sure enough, a bright red cardinal swooped by the window. I briefly told my sister and brother-in-law about the chirping cardinal of the night before, but we all had other things on our minds right then.

That sad day lumbered on. Hospice came, the hearse came, relatives came. We made arrangements, we picked out clothes for our mother, and then Joe and I drove home. Now it was Sunday afternoon, still the same day my mother left us. Exhausted, Joe and I crawled into bed for naps. The cats joined us as the wind picked up outside. A storm was brewing in the southwest.

But I could not sleep. I began to feel panicky. I had never been in this world without my mother. She and I talked to each other almost every day of my life, and now I could never again even call her on the phone. I gave up on the nap and got up.

I walked through the house, looked out the windows, and cried. It slowly dawned on me that in all this activity of Mom's illness and death, I hadn't noticed that spring had come and gone. We were already on the cusp of summer. Seven huge maple trees, each four stories high, stood guard around the west and north sides of the farmhouse, and they were fully leafed out. Now their branches and leaves moved wildly in the warm wind.

I figured there was still time before the storm would hit, so I moved to the patio where I could cry without waking Joe, and I sank into a wicker chair. The sky in the west was deep gray and turbulent. The maple leaves moving in the wind were getting noisier by the minute, and those high branches creaked. Birds had apparently taken cover. I listened and watched, and I cried. It seemed that nature was expressing my feelings.

And then I heard it. Over the sound of the trees in the wind was a loud chirping. I looked up, and there in those majestic maples was a male cardinal. He swooped from tree to tree, in and out of the green branches. He was the only bird out there that I could see or hear, and he was noisy and bright red against all that green. In spite of the approaching storm, he seemed to be doing what he was born to do. It's not just that he seemed fearless; he was having an absolute blast, as if this were his own personal playground. I watched him soar and swoop and dance around in the heavy air of this approaching storm. I listened to him chirp over the sound of the wind. For the first time in days, I felt my stomach unknot.

I suddenly knew that somehow, some way, this was from my mother. It had been so the night before, it had been so this morning, and it was now. I was being brought comfort, and I felt assured right down to my toes that my mother was free of the virtual cage of aging and illness that kept her from moving and talking. I also knew without a doubt that she was not lost to me forever, that I would join her someday.

How long did I sit there? I'm not sure. But while I watched that flying, dancing, noisy, beautiful bird, I stopped crying.

The next morning, I rose early and went to my computer to write the eulogy for Mom's funeral. While I sat at the keyboard, I heard the chirping. I looked out my window, and there on the south lawn—a lawn with no trees—the red cardinal stood in the grass, as vocal as ever. He was framed in the only window in the room. I felt comforted and went back to my writing.

For the next couple of days, the cardinal hung around the house, mostly in the yews. It began to feel natural to see this little guy. I actually sat next to an open window once and talked to him, and he stayed right there, perched on a yew branch, cocking his head at me, chirping.

As the week went on, however, the cardinal moved farther and farther away. No longer did he sit on the yews next to the window. Sometimes I could hear him but not see him. I had the sense that my mother was moving farther away from me.

Then I had a vivid dream.

In the dream, my mother called on the phone from the next life to assure me. Her voice sounded young and happy, and I could hear her smile as she talked. I started crying, and I told her how much I missed her. She cooed in her motherly way. She told me that she was the cardinal. "I wasn't sure if I should be a yellow bird or a red one, but I decided to go with red," she said, and that sounded so much like her.

The day before, I had covered her grave with red rose petals, and I told her about it in the dream. She said she knew, and she raved at how beautiful the roses were. I asked her what she was trying to say to us on that last day when she could not talk, but she gently indicated that I could not ask about her time with us.

She had an almost secretive happiness, like someone who is engaged or pregnant but not telling anyone yet. I said, "You're not quite gone away, are you?" She said that was true, but she was almost gone. She gave me a phone number I could try at a certain time to reach her, though she couldn't guarantee she'd be there. I started to feel panic because I was losing her smiling voice. Then the connection broke up. I hung up and tried the number, and it would not work. Then I woke up.

That was one week to the day since Mom had died. My friend Jeanette came over for Sunday dinner. After we ate, Joe left us alone, and Jeanette and I took our iced teas to the patio. It was a stunning day, and the birds were vocal in the maples. I decided to take the risk and tell my friend about the cardinal.

Jeanette was very moved, and she agreed that the bird was a messenger of some kind. Then I told her my dream of the night before. This was the first I'd talked about it, and when I finished, Jeanette said, "Listen . . ."

Up in the trees was the bold chirping of one cardinal, louder than all the other bird sounds. Jeanette and I looked at each other, then we tried to find him. We followed his chirp all around the seven maples in the yard, and although we both heard him loud and clear, neither of us was able to catch sight of him. The next day I no longer heard him.

The year anniversary of my mother's death came on a Monday. I dreaded its arrival, but it turned out that I would be hosting a meeting in my house all that day. I was grateful people would be around. I woke up that morning to a steady, gentle rain that would last all day.

Joe and I had left the farmhouse a few months before and moved to a small house in the next county. No more towering maples, but we did have apple trees and willow trees in the yard and lots of windows. My guests remarked on the windows, and we had our meeting.

Something so sweet happened that day that I asked the others to verify what I saw. In the backyard, then the front yard, then the backyard again, back and forth, a flock of cardinals, both male and female, played in the light rain. All day. On the first anniversary of my mother's death, I was not alone in any way. God sent me perfect comfort.

About the Contributors

DeVonna R. Allison is a freelance writer and speaker whose work has been featured in a variety of books, magazines, and online publications. Her work has been included in several different anthologies, including three Chicken Soup for the Soul books. She and her husband of forty-plus years are both Marine Corps veterans, and after thirty-four years in the Midwest, raising their four children, they currently make their home in central Florida. Now they enjoy visits with their grandchildren, trips to the local beaches, working in their flower beds, and volunteering in veterans organizations. Her webpage can be found at DeVonna RAllisonAuthor.wordpress.com.

Catherine Ulrich Brakefield is an award-winning author and ardent lover of Christ, as well as a hopeless romantic and patriot. She skillfully intertwines these elements into her writing (*Wilted Dandelions* and the Destiny Series: *Swept into Destiny, Destiny's Whirlwind, Destiny of Heart,* and *Waltz with Destiny*). Her newest book is the inspirational Amish futuristic romance, *Love's Final Sunrise.* She is a longtime Michigan resident and married to her husband for over forty-five years and has two adult children and four grandchildren. For more information about Catherine, see CatherineUlrichBrakefield.com.

Rose McCormick Brandon is the author of the devotional *Rooted: Daily Learning the Ways of Jesus* and *Promises of Home: Stories of Canada's British Home Children*, as well as other books and numerous published articles. Rose is an avid student of the Scriptures and enjoys writing and teaching Bible studies. Rose and husband, Doug, live in Caledonia, Ontario, and have three adult children and five grandchildren, whom they love to spend as much time with as possible.

Melody Carlson is the award-winning author of more than 250 books with sales of more than 7.5 million, including many bestselling Christmas novellas, young adult titles, and contemporary romances. She received a *Romantic Times* Career Achievement Award, her novel *All Summer Long* has been made into a Hallmark movie, and the movie based on her novel *The Happy Camper* premiered on UPtv in 2023. She and her husband live in central Oregon.

Born and raised in Kentucky, **Betty L. Carter** published four Appalachian fiction and nonfiction books. She wrote what she knew. She is an author, poet, singer, and songwriter, having written hundreds of songs. Betty received her Bachelor of Human Services and Counseling at age fifty-nine. She is the mother of four, grandmother of eight, and great-grandmother of seven. Betty feels her family is the most important part of her life.

Andrea Doering is an editor, wife, mother of three, and a contributor to publications such as Guideposts *Strength and Grace* and The Upper Room.

Lynn Dove is an award-winning author and freelance writer with articles published in several magazines and anthologies, including Chicken Soup for the Soul books. Her blog, *Journey Thoughts*, is a Canadian Christian Writing Award winner and has a worldwide following. She lives in Cochrane, Alberta, Canada, with her husband and dotes on her eight grandbabies every chance she gets!

Chrissy Drzewiecki lives in the southern valley of East Tennessee with her darlin' Mike and their six-year-old pup, Tanner. This is her fourth published story in Revell anthologies, and she has been published in eight other anthologies. She is currently writing a screenplay with her son, adapted from her novel in progress. She would love to hear from you at ChrissyDrew.com or at Facebook.com/AuthorChrissyDrew.

Lonnie Hull DuPont (1953–2023) was an accomplished and award-winning author and editor; an amazing writer and poet; a lover of cats, dogs, horses, and other four-legged creatures; a lover of art in all its forms; and a hip and stylish urban dweller with her heart tied to the countryside. Her books include *She Calls the Moon by Its Name: Poems*, *Kit Kat and Lucy*, and *The Haiku Box*. Her poetry can also be read in dozens of periodicals and literary journals.

Lonnie's memorial bench (photo on dedication page) is located in Sparks Foundation County Park (a.k.a. Cascades Park) in Jackson, Michigan. The easiest way to visit it is to park your vehicle on Brown Street across from The Cascades (1401 South Brown Street, Jackson, Michigan 49203) and then walk east on the dirt path that goes straight through the middle of the lagoon.

After teaching reading and writing for forty-six and a half years, **Maureen M. Elwyn** decided to retire and write her own stories.

She prefers to write creative nonfiction, especially about her childhood growing up on a wildlife refuge in Monkey's Eyebrow, Kentucky, as well as a few stories featuring ancestors past and present. She and her husband, Paul, have called Danville, Kentucky, their home since 1975. Their daughter, Laura, lives nearby with her husband, George, and their three pets. When not writing, Maureen teaches the art of crafting memoir to adults while encouraging them to share their memories with family and friends.

Glenda Ferguson has education degrees from College of the Ozarks and Indiana University. She has contributed to Chicken Soup for the Soul, the Short and Sweet series, and *Second Chance Horses*. For *All God's Creatures*, Glenda writes devotions about pets, animals, and the birds of Indiana. Her writing encouragement comes from the Writers Forum of Burton Kimble Farms Education Center. As a volunteer with Indiana Landmarks, she conducts tours of two historical hotels. Glenda and her husband, Tim, live on an acre in southern Indiana with their two cats, Speckles and Scrappy.

Allison Lynn Flemming is drawn to the power of story to grow hearts and communities. As a singer, songwriter, and worship leader, Allison and her husband, Gerald Flemming, form the award-winning duo Infinitely More. Their ninth album—*The Sum of All Love*—explores the joys and challenges of living an authentic life of faith. Allison writes devotionals, songs, articles, and creative nonfiction to remind people how deeply they are loved by God. Her writings have appeared in *All God's Creatures* (Guideposts), The Upper Room (devotionals), Warner Press (devotionals), and include six stories with Chicken Soup for the Soul. Find Allison at InfinitelyMore.ca.

Gerald Flemming wrote his first songs when he was seven. He wrote stories and poetry through his teens. His first play was produced when he was eighteen. He studied playwriting at the National Theatre School. After having ten plays produced, he returned to his first love, music. He and his wife, Allison, moved to Nashville, where he wrote 230 songs, some with Grammy nominees/winners and Dove Award winners. They moved back to Canada and formed the musical ministry Infinitely More. They've been nominated for fifteen national music awards. Their album, *The Beauty of the One*, won two GMA Awards.

Susy Flory is the *New York Times* bestselling author or coauthor of seventeen books. Her most recent book, *Sanctuary* (Tyndale, 2022), coauthored with Patrick Barrett, is the true story of an Irish village, a man who lost his way, and the rescue donkeys that led him home. Susy's 2014 book with Scott LeRette, *The Unbreakable Boy*, was recently made into a major motion picture by Lionsgate Studios. Susy loves animals and being outdoors and often pitches in to help her daughter with wildlife rescue in the squirrel nursery at their house in the mountains.

Karen Foster speaks at women's church events and has written multiple articles and devotions. She's the author of the nonfiction narrative book *Lunch with Loretta: Discover the Power of a Mentoring Friendship*. Karen has contributed to several anthologies, including *The Horse of My Dreams*, *The Cat in the Christmas Tree*, and *Chicken Soup for the Soul: Military Families*.

Jane Gwaltney was born on Travis Air Force Base and grew up in St. Louis, Missouri. She's a member of Writers Under the Arch. She was blessed with parents who encouraged her talents as a writer and artist. By example, they also gifted her with a reverence for family and deep respect for all living beings with feathers, fur, and fins.

Award-winning author **Melissa Henderson** writes inspirational messages sometimes humming with humor. With stories online and in print publications, Melissa hopes to encourage readers. Melissa is the author of *Licky the Lizard* and *Grumpy the Gator.* Her passions are helping in the community and church. Melissa is an elder, deacon, and Stephen Minister. Follow Melissa on Facebook, Twitter, Pinterest, Instagram, Goodreads, BookBub, YouTube, LinkedIn, and at www.MelissaGHenderson.com.

Lee Juslin graduated from Bucknell University and received a master's degree from Fairleigh Dickinson University. She is a retired copywriter and lives in New Bern, North Carolina, with her husband, Scott, and four cats. She owns an embroidery business, I B Dog Gone, which she uses to support a number of breed rescues. She is the author of several children's books based on her Scottish terrier, a certified therapy dog, the late, great Nurse Frosty. She also contributes terrier rescue articles to *Kings River Life Magazine.*

Jenny Lynn Keller is an award-winning author who transforms her family's rowdy adventures into stories filled with hope, humor, and plenty of Southern charm. Follow their fun on her blog at JennyLynnKeller.com and Facebook.com/JennyLynn Keller. Her beloved true animal stories appear in Callie Smith Grant's compilations *The Horse of My Dreams, The Dog Who Came to Christmas, The Cat in the Christmas Tree,* and *Second-Chance Horses.*

Thomas Kienzle is a retired scientist who now enjoys a mostly stress-free life by chasing his passions of nature photography, fishing, and writing. He has published one nonfiction book, *Rabies* (2007). He has also had several short stories published in the following anthologies: *Tales from the South, Writing on the Walls, Precious, Precocious Moments,* and *Elmwood Stories to Die For.*

Sherry Diane Kitts, originally from southwest Virginia near the Blue Ridge Mountains, currently resides with her husband in central Florida. Sherry writes nonfiction short stories and devotions and has been published in several anthologies. She belongs to Word Weavers International and writes from her life's adventures. Sherry hopes others receive joy and encouragement as they read and relate to her experiences.

David Kitz is a Bible dramatist, an award-winning author, and a conference speaker. He serves as an ordained outreach minister with the Foursquare Gospel Church of Canada. His love for storytelling and drama is evident to all who have seen his Bible-based performances. For several years, he has toured across the continent with a variety of one-man plays for both children and adults. Though raised on a farm on the Canadian prairies, David now lives with his wife, Karen, in Canada's capital, Ottawa. They have two adult sons, Timothy and Joshua, and a daughter-in-law, Jasmine.

Marci Kladnik is an award-winning writer and photographer. She has won multiple Muse medallions, Certificates of Excellence, and the 2015 Kari Winters Rescue and Advocacy Award from the Cat Writers' Association. She was a finalist for a Maxwell from the Dog Writers Association of America. For seven years she wrote a biweekly newspaper column about feral cats while sitting on the board of Catalyst for Cats, Inc. Her work has been published in books and magazines and in various online and print publications. In addition, she authored two children's books about her Scottie and a feral kitten. Marci served as president of the Cat Writers' Association for four years. She moved from sunny California to Wisconsin, where she lives with her dog and two cats, all rescues.

Wendy Klopfenstein enjoys sunshine, sweet tea, and a good book, preferably all at the same time. Having always loved creating stories as much as reading them, she now puts the ones wandering around in her head on paper for others to enjoy. When she's not sitting on the porch reading, you can find her working on her next novel. For more information on her books, you can visit her website at WendyKlopfenstein.com.

Mary Beth Laufer earned a degree in English education from SUNY Albany. She has contributed poems, essays, and stories to several periodicals and to over fifty anthologies, including eighteen different versions of Chicken Soup for the Soul. Her middle-grade novel, *Katelyn's Crow*, explores the ethical treatment of all wildlife, and in 2023 it was awarded a Kirkus Star. Laufer lives in Central Florida, where she's writing a sequel called *Katelyn's Cat* and teachers' guides to both books.

Karen M. Leet from Lexington, Kentucky, loves her family, friends, animals, and above all else the Lord. A lifelong writer, she's published hundreds of stories and articles and a middle-grade historical novel, *Sarah's Courage*, from the History Press.

Andi Lehman freelances as a writer of nonfiction stories, articles, devotions, and educational programs. She is grateful to have worked for years with dear friend and editor Lonnie Hull DuPont and to be working now with Lonnie's successor and like-minded editor Andrea Doering. A passionate advocate for the value of all animals, Andi teaches the wonder of God's creatures (and our responsibility to them) through her education company, Life with Animals. To learn more about Andi's commitment to words and critters—including her children's book entitled *Saving Schmiddy*—please visit AndiLehman.com.

Nicole M. Miller lives in Washington State with her husband and children, along with her horses, chickens, ducks, dogs, cats, and guinea pigs. See more of her stories in *The Horse of My Heart, The Horse of My Dreams, The Dog Who Came to Christmas,* and *Second-Chance Horses.* Her debut novel, *Until Our Time Comes: A Novel of WWII Poland,* was published with Revell in 2024. Learn more at NicoleMillerWriter.com.

DJ Perry's ability to weave a tight story with complex themes and multilayered characters has resulted in a dozen-plus of his scripts being produced into award-winning feature films. Other writers have novelized DJ's screenplays into books such as *Ghost Town* (Bob Terrell), *Wild Michigan* (Dee Freeman), and *Knight Chills* (David Hayes). In addition to DJ's original screenplays, he's adapted two Karl Manke books (*Hope from Heaven* and *Harsens Island Revenge*) into screenplays and films. DJ has also been a contributing author on four books focusing on animals published by Revell. He resides in Michigan, where he continues a career in filmmaking in front of and behind the camera.

Patricia Avery Pursley is a retired freelance media-relations agent who represented authors and wrote a boatload of press material for nearly twenty years. Her amusing stories have been published in the books *The Cat in the Christmas Tree* and *Second-Chance Cats.* Living in The Woodlands, Texas, with husband, Tom, and rescue cat Princey, she writes, attempts to keep plants alive through heat and cold, and is a volunteer at large for The

Woodlands Arts Council. Patricia and Tom might be found wandering distant shores and evaluating key lime pie.

Barbara Ragsdale is an award-winning writer of short stories. She is published in the Chicken Soup anthologies and eleven short-story collections published by CC Writers. Other writing credits include "A Walking Miracle" in *Miracles Do Happen*, published by Guideposts, "Can, Sir," a poem published in *Final Moments*, and a WWII veteran interview in *Forever Young*. Her poem "How Will He Know He Is Beautiful?" was published by *Long Story Short* ezine magazine. She has received writing awards from SouthWest Writers and the Memphis Public Library. She was a staff writer of author interviews for *Southern Writers* magazine. When not writing, she is an exercise instructor with the Silver Sneakers program.

Lauraine Snelling is the award-winning author of more than one hundred books, fiction and nonfiction, for adults and young adults. Her books have sold more than five million copies. She makes her home in Tehachapi, California. Learn more at Lau raineSnelling.com.

Joan Soggie is a mom, a grandma, and a great-grandmother. She and her husband, Dennis, have lived and farmed in the Saskatchewan prairie for the past sixty years. The land and its creatures are her passion, and her family is her joy. She hopes to spend the rest of her days in the same place, sharing experiences with family and friends, human or other. She loves telling their stories.

Claudia Wolfe St. Clair is an artist, writer, retired art therapist, and anam cara from Toledo, Ohio. She is the mother of three and grandmother of six. She and the love of her life, Alan Imhoff, have restored the family home and gardens on the shore of Lake Erie. You can read more from Claudia in the Callie Grant Smith collections *Second-Chance Horses, The Horse of My Dreams, The Horse of My Heart, Second-Chance Dogs, Second-Chance Cats, The Dog Who Came to Christmas,* and *The Cat in the Christmas Tree.*

Delores E. Topliff grew up in Washington State but married a Canadian so enjoys dual citizenship. She teaches university, travels, and writes children's books, historic novels, and a fun memoir of her many trips to Israel. She loves her two doctor sons and five grandchildren and divides her year between a Minnesota farm and the gentler climate of northeastern Mississippi. Find her at DeloresTopliff.com and Facebook.com/DETopliff.

Katelyn Van Kooten is a children's author and freelance writer who works in the publishing industry. She lives in Grand Rapids, Michigan, and can often be found watching birds, reading a novel, or drinking too much coffee. Find her on Instagram @KVKWriter.

Susan M. Watkins is an award-winning, multi-published author who wrote for *The 700 Club* television program and a variety of international CBN websites. Her work is featured in numerous books, and she's authored several columns. Entering her first writing competition at age eleven, Susan secured first place, igniting her literary passion. She's best described as "a literary artist painting with the stroke of a pen" whose focus remains centered on those seeking a fresh perspective on life. Additional publishing credits include Grammy Award winner Gloria Gaynor's *We Will Survive* and a Max Lucado evangelistic website.

Notes

1. Robert Farrar Capon, *The Supper of the Lamb* (Harcourt Brace Jovanovich, 1967), 146–47.

2. Peter Harris, *Under the Bright Wings* (Regent College Publishing, 2000), 36.

3. Herbert Lockyer, *All the Promises of the Bible* (Zondervan, 1962).

A Note from the Publisher

Dear Reader,

Thank you for selecting a Revell book! We're so happy to be part of your life through this work.

Revell's mission is to publish books that offer hope and help for meeting life's challenges, and that bring comfort and inspiration. We know that the right words at the right time can make all the difference; it is our goal with every title to provide just the words you need.

We believe in building lasting relationships with readers, and we'd love to get to know you better. If you have any feedback, questions, or just want to chat about your experience reading this book, please email us directly at publisher@revellbooks.com. Your insights are incredibly important to us, and it would be our pleasure to hear how we can better serve you.

We look forward to hearing from you and having the chance to enhance your experience with Revell Books.

The Publishing Team at Revell Books
A Division of Baker Publishing Group
publisher@revellbooks.com

Revell